DATES AND TIME

a handbook for local historians

British Association for Local History

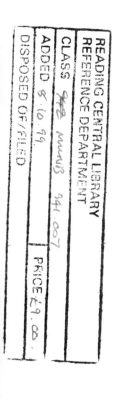

Published by British Association for Local History
24 Lower Street, Harnham SALISBURY SP2 8EY

ISBN 1 86077 074 6

First edition, 1997

(BALH General Editor: Alan G. Crosby)

Designed and printed by Salisbury Printing Company Limited
Greencroft Street SALISBURY SP1 1JF

Front cover: Hiram Taylor, 'knocker-up' of Oswaldtwistle (see page 39)

CONTENTS

LIST OF ILLUSTRATIONS

Picture acknowledgements
The author and publisher are very grateful to the following for their kind permission to reproduce illustrations used in this book: Science Museum/Science and Society Picture Library (nos. 1, 3-5, 10, 11, 13-17, 23, 24, 29 and 30); St Albans Museum (no. 2); Alan Crosby (no. 8); the Trustees of Sir John Soane's Museum (no. 9); John Bynoe (no. 12); National Railway Museum/Science and Society Picture Library (no. 18); Frank Watson of Accrington (no. 19); the Suffolk Record Office (no. 26).

ACKNOWLEDGEMENTS

This booklet began its life with a suggestion from Dr Alan Crosby that I might write 'an introduction and guide to the dating of documents and historical sources ... a simple distillation of Cheney's *Handbook of Dates*, accessible to newcomers'. I began trying to produce something on these lines and discussed my ideas with David Dymond and Peter Northeast. This led me to suggest that simplifying Cheney was not practical, but a booklet 'explaining how to use Cheney [and] describing how human societies, and historians, have come to measure time' might be useful. This, 'while primarily of use to the local and family historian, could be so written as to be valuable to teachers of history generally'. This is what I have tried to produce.

Needless to say I have depended heavily on the publications listed in the bibliography *and* on *Whitaker's Almanack 1997* and the *Encyclopaedia Britannica*. Dr Alan Crosby has made innumerable invaluable suggestions. Peter Northeast has provided me with almost all the specific medieval information; David Dymond has allowed me to use his own notes on the ritual year. Dr John Alexander has suggested improvements to the archaeological sections. Barry Landy has been kind enough to check thoroughly and correct my Appendix 5. Dr J. H. Bettey has given me information about local adjustments to Greenwich time in Bristol and Oxford. I am grateful to them all. David Dymond and Peter Northeast have combed my text for errors and much improved it. The errors which remain are mine.

LMM
Cambridge 1997

Whenever I have referred to Cheney's *Handbook* I have put the page numbers in square brackets in the text, to save repetitive footnotes. I have done the same with Biblical quotations. In some quotations I have omitted words and phrases but have <u>not</u> changed the sense. My attention was drawn, when the text was finished, to the invaluable information in the sections of *Whitaker's Almanack 1997* on 'Astronomy' and on 'Time Measurement and Calendars'. While presented from a different point of view, concerned with the present and future rather than the past, this can be extremely useful to local and family historians. I have, therefore, given detailed references to relevant passages in footnotes and in the Appendices.

EDITOR'S FOREWORD

The need to establish precise and accurate dates for the creation of documents, maps and other written sources is fundamental to the methodology of local history. We need to be able to place events in their proper order, and therefore must place documents and other sources in a comparable chronological order, and also need to establish the context of an event, a process, a specific source – how does the material or event which we are studying fit into the pattern of time and events in the wider world. At the end of the 20th century this has become an intrinsic part of existence. How often do we – probably subconsciously – glance at a wristwatch, listen to the timechecks on radio or television, look at the digital displays of time beside the bed, on a computer screen, high on a wall in an airport or station? How often are our actions governed by the need to conform to a timetable at work, when travelling, in learning or even in the way we organise our leisure. To us, time and its measurement are inextricable from every aspect of living.

We are also ever aware of the passing of time. Comparison with the past is a preoccupation of our age, not only in terms of society's love affair with 'heritage', but as we measure the present in relation to what has gone before. The breaking of records for weather or the price of paintings, the longevity or short duration of the lives of individuals great and ordinary, the perception of science and technological achievement in terms of progression and development – all these indicate a constant awareness of time and its passing. And the role which history itself plays in our cultural life, whether as TV drama, the investigations of our family origins, or the publicity shots of Beefeaters at the Tower on tourist board ephemera, emphasises the knowledge of the unfolding of time which is part of our cultural inheritance.

But 'twas not always thus. As Lionel Munby so clearly indicates in this book, awareness of time is not something inherent in human beings, but something which has been developed as cultural change has taken place. People in the past did not necessarily think of time and history in the way in which we do, and many were largely unaware of such concepts. When we undertake historical research we must be aware that the values of the end of the 20th century were not those of individuals three or four hundred years ago. They perceived time differently, measured it differently, and used it differently. Their dating systems were not those which we use today, and the means of measuring divisions of time were limited, often inaccurate, and probably irrelevant to most people.

The first part of this book discusses these issues, so that local historians and others can begin to appreciate just what 'time' and 'date' may have meant in the past. It also shows how historians can use older dating methods, such as regnal years, to ascribe dates to documents which they are studying, and elucidates confusing topics such as the date of New Year's Day and the Julian and Gregorian calendars. The second part comprises a series of detailed appendices which tabulate the regnal years, other calendars, saints' days and similar information of importance to local historians. As General Editor for the British Association for Local History, I would like to thank the author, Lionel Munby, for producing such a detailed and comprehensive volume which will be welcomed by local historians everywhere.

Alan G. Crosby

ABOUT THE AUTHOR

LIONEL MUNBY was Staff Tutor to the Board of Extra-Mural Studies of the University of Cambridge from 1946 to 1982, and was James Stuart Lecturer from 1980 to 1985. Working with various adult groups in Cambridge and Hertfordshire he produced and edited parish histories, and has also edited the following books: *East Anglian Studies* (1968), *Life and Death in Kings Langley* (1981) and *Early Stuart Household Accounts* (1986). In 1977 his *Hertfordshire Landscape* was published; in 1994 he contributed the essay on 'Hertfordshire' to *English County Histories: a Tribute to C.R. Elrington*; and in 1995 *The Common People are Not Nothing 1575-1780*, studies of Hertfordshire history, was published. For 20 years (1955-75) he edited *The Local Historian*, the quarterly journal of the Standing Conference for Local History (now the British Association for Local History), and from 1961-71 also edited *Short Guides to Records*, published by the Historical Association. In 1988 he produced *Reading Tudor and Stuart Handwriting* and in 1989 *How Much is that Worth?* (second edition 1996), both of which were published by B.A.L.H. He retired officially in 1982 but is still occupied writing and, occasionally, teaching and travelling. *Hertfordshire in History*, a collection of papers, was presented to him in 1991. He became President of B.A.L.H. in 1995.

1. A working model of a Chinese waterwheel escapement of about AD1080; the original would have been fitted to an astronomical clock.

2. St Albans clock tower: the only medieval town belfry to survive in England, the tower was built by Thomas Wolvey, formerly the Royal Mason, at the beginning of the 15th century. It was sited on high ground in the centre of the town, looking across to - and indeed challenging - the abbey, so that the town could sound its own hours. This illustration shows the tower in the early 19th century, with shops built around its base.

1

INTRODUCTION

'To think of time—of all that retrospection!
To think of today, and the ages continued henceforward!
Is today nothing? Is the beginningless past nothing?'
[*Walt Whitman, 'To Think of Time', in* Leaves of Grass, *(London 1907), pp 385 &*
387]

The very essence of history is to fix events in order of time. Historians seek to
explain change through time, but what is time? The *Concise Oxford Dictionary*
[8th edition] has almost two columns devoted to 'time'. Nineteen definitions of
the noun, five of the verb, and sixty-two examples of phrases and idioms must
make this one of the longest entries. Yet to most people what matters is the
present. For centuries ordinary working people measured the passage of time
by the natural cycle of the seasons and by natural work rhythms. There emerged
an annual calendar of religious and secular festivals related to these regularly
recurring experiences. The consciousness, and consequently the measurement,
of past time is a specialised interest. Recording the passage of time has been, in
the main, the concern of 'the gentry, the masters, the farmers and the
tradesmen'.[1] This interest became stronger from the sixteenth century. Perhaps
the development of humanist ideas in the Renaissance increased the
individual's perception of him/herself as an incident in time? This is when
diaries, recording passing events and current feelings, proliferate, as do
biographies and autobiographies. The Heralds' *Visitations* and the beginning of
local histories based largely on genealogy and the 'descent of the manor'
suggest a growing interest in what came before the present. The past acquired
an aura; it had been a 'Golden Age', the 'Garden of Eden', and today the 'good
old days'.

The current publicity over the Millennium might suggest that interest in the
future is new. If anything it is as old as interest in the past. People living in the
tenth century were extremely conscious of the first millennium, on which
religious fantasies as wild as any of today's were focussed. We are, however,
more conscious of the future than were earlier generations. 'Current events'
are discussed in the media with constant emphasis on what is going to happen
as a result of this or that present development. Before the present century
Utopias were usually set in the past, whether sited in Britain or somewhere
else in the world. Modern Utopias have tended to be sited in the future or, as
in the case of much science fiction, in the mythical future of outer space.

The claim by David Landes that 'what matters to the ordinary man is that he
can measure time' explains the subject matter of this booklet, and how it has
been written.[2]

3. Measuring the passage of time: Plaster cast of an Egyptian water 'clock' of 1480-1415 BC: the original was found at Karnak in 1904. Water leaked slowly, and at a measured rate, through a small hole in the base of the 'bucket' and time was indicated by the water level. Such a 'clock' showed only the passing of time, not the time itself.

4. A candle clock: as in the previous illustration, a candle clock showed only the passing of time, burning down at a steady rate with hourly intervals marked on the wax of the candle itself.

5. Four sand glasses, made in Italy about 1720: they are the familiar double phials of glass, mounted in a frame of ebony and ivory. The glasses are marked with quarter-hour time intervals of 1/4, 2/4 , 3/4 and 4/4 indicated by the number of studs set above and below each glass in the enclosing panels. The principle is exactly the same as the egg-timers which were widely used until recent years.

2

DATING

Do dates matter?

There was a time when most history teaching, at least for children in school, meant learning dates. That has long ceased to be so, for what seemed good reasons. What used to be learnt, with the help of jingles, were items like the progression of English kings from the Norman Conquest.

'Willie, Willie, Harry, Ste,
Harry, Dick, John, Harry Three'

with the dates, all learnt by heart: 1066 to 1087, 1087 to 1100, 1100 to 1135 and so on. The dates of battles came next in priority: Crecy (1346), Agincourt (1415), Bosworth (1485), the Armada (1588), Blenheim (1704), Trafalgar (1805). Then Acts of Parliament: 1707 the Union; 1832 Parliamentary Reform. More in keeping with modern thinking was the learning of the dates of inventions, for example: Spinning Jenny (1764); Steam Engine (1775). But how often were children, or adults for that matter, really taught what the inventions were for?

There were several reasons for the reaction against this kind of learning by rote: learning 'facts' by heart without understanding the nature of the society to which they were relevant is useless. Too much emphasis on a few dates can give the impression that everything changed in those years, that the past was abruptly divided up into very widely different periods of time. For example, more important than the year of the invention is the period of time over which it came into general use. The modern ball point pen provides a good instance: as the *Independent* noted on 8 December 1995, 'a primitive version dates back to 1895. The breakthrough came in 1938 when Laszlo Biro developed and patented the workable prototype of a blot-free pen. The biro hit the shops of Britain in the run-up to Christmas 1945, this was a luxury purchase at 55s. Yet within four years [it] was outselling old-fashioned fountain pens'. Which is the key date?

The traditional dates, the 'facts', inculcated a one-sided view of history. After the Second World War there was a reaction and many new ways of teaching history were popularised; they had in common the aim of bringing an understanding of the nature of past societies, presenting them in the round, often with the emphasis on ordinary people. This could be just as one-sided, if more acceptable. What was common to most of this teaching was a *relative* indifference to dates.

Those who learnt history a generation or two ago had a kind of road map through time, with dates as sign posts, markers. They may have been poor ones but without some framework of dates into which to fit past events it is impossible to understand cause and effect in historical development. A newspaper once described a film, 'The Deep Concern', as 'largely filmed at Stanford Hall in Leicestershire, a beautiful William and Mary house mentioned in Domesday Book'. Dr Alan Crosby has come across 'a restaurant which is mentioned in Domesday Book'! Such ignorance makes for a nonsense. There are too many school children today who do not know that the Romans came before the Normans. So historians must have date charts, though there may be argument over which dates ought to go into them. What IS important is to ensure that the chosen dates are accurate; that is not always easy.

The *Anglo-Saxon Chronicle* is the earliest considerable record of dates in English history. The reconstructed modern text is compiled from seven different manuscripts, some of which have different years for the same event. Dorothy Whitelock, editor of an up to date version, describes the problem: 'it is not always possible to decide if one text is in error, or if they are using different styles of beginning the year'.[3] We will see later the reasons for this. For the moment it emphasises the difficulty the student has in discovering the accurate date of an event.

Modern scholars can slip up. A comparison of S. H. Steinberg's *Historical Tables*, G. R. Elton's *Reform and Reformation*, and J. Scarisbrick's *Henry VIII* reveals some surprising contradictions. Cardinal Wolsey's fall in 1529 is dated variously, as follows: 'Oct 17: Fall of Lord Chancellor Wolsey'; 'the cardinal surrendered the great seal on the 18th [October]. On the 22nd he surrendered himself and all his possessions'; 'Two days later [than 20 September] came the command to hand over the great seal. After an argument Wolsey surrendered his seal'. The same three authors have different dates for one of Henry VIII's marriages. The marriage with Anne of Cleves was declared void in 1540, on 6 July by Steinberg, 9 July by Scarisbrick, and on 10 July by Elton. Catherine Howard's marriage took place in the same year, on 28 July according to Scarisbrick and Steinberg, and on 9 August according to Elton.[4] G. D. H. Cole gave different dates for the same events in two of his own books. Two incidents are reversed in time. In one book he wrote that in 1887 'many were injured ... the day came to be known as "Bloody Sunday" ... other meetings followed, and at one in 1888 a workman named Linnell was killed'. In another book he stated that 'Alfred Linnell died of injuries received from the police in November 1887' and 'Bloody Sunday' followed in 1888.[5]

Occasionally such errors may be misprints due to inadequate proof corrections but more often they occur because even the most illustrious historians have copied from others without checking the original source. This has sometimes perpetuated an error in publication after publication. More commonly mistakes arise because the forms in which original documents have been dated have changed over time and place in ways which are quite unfamiliar to people today. All local and family historians learn this painfully. The source from which the best guidance comes is C. R. Cheney's *Handbook of*

Dates, first published in 1945 by the Royal Historical Society and still in print. This invaluable book is not easy for the beginner to use and one of the purposes of this present book is to help the student to use Cheney. The other intention is to provide a wider study of dating methods.

Relative dating

The changes in a society with little or no written history, its creations, its culture and its artefacts, cannot be understood until their relative position in time is known. Historians and pre-historians of all kinds have wrestled with dating and sought to improve the techniques relevant to their specialism in order to make their dating more accurate. Such dating starts with discovering the association, or connection in time, of similar and dissimilar events or objects, and becomes ever more precise with the increase of knowledge and the development of new techniques. Archaeologists in the nineteenth century in Europe, for example, invented terms such as the Stone, Bronze, and Iron Ages, based on the successive and improving materials used in tool making, to which 'Ages' they gave boundaries in time, but these proved inapplicable in many parts of the world. A global chronology only became possible with radiocarbon and other absolute dating methods whereby events in time became much more precisely defined.[6]

6. Tree rings: the illustration shows how the rings vary in thickness depending on the growing conditions in a particular season. It is such variations in pattern which are used, rather like a bar chart, to estimate the age of timbers taken from old buildings. By using numerous such samples archaeologists and historians have been able to produce 'composite' pattern charts which can be used as a measure against which to date specific examples.

Sir Crispin Tickell has outlined the 'astonishing amount of knowledge [which] has been put together, mostly within the last few years ... the new range of scientific techniques for dating the past, measurement of the varying isotopes of carbon 14, uranium-thorium, potassium argon, and so on has transformed chronology ... Then there are datable variations in lake and river deposits; datable deposits of pollens, animals (in particular insects), and plants to demonstrate the nature of past ecosystems; and variations in rock magnetism in sedimentary deposits. Short-term historical evidence is also available: ... variations in tree rings [dendrochronology], the dates of wine harvests year after year, and the advances and retreats of glaciers; [even] the dates in Kyoto for cherry blossom'.[7] With dendrochronology it was even possible to date building timber almost to a particular year. Cecil Hewett's careful study of timber joints in Essex buildings, in barns, belfries, doors, naves, porches and spires, enabled him to put them in relative time order and so to date many buildings: 'If my suggestions are acceptable, it follows that buildings incorporating techniques or joints identical with any described in this sequence, can be dated by such joints'.[8] When Thomas Rickman (1776–1841) suggested that the different styles of English 'Gothic' church buildings were due to changes over time, to their relative dates, and not the product of individual whims (1817), he made it possible to understand how the successive styles evolved from one another and so date the building of churches. These were classic examples of how relative dating advanced historical knowledge.

Historians have dated documents by the handwriting which changed, for example, between the thirteenth and fourteenth centuries. In the seventeenth century what has been called Secretary Hand, the common hand of the ordinary person, was moving towards more modern letter formations. One sometimes finds documents of the same period in substantially different handwriting. It is easy to see which one was written by an older person, whose writing was learnt much earlier. Changing fashions in the teaching of handwriting in our own time can give away when a particular individual was at school. Relative dating, arranging historical material in time order, is the first stage in achieving an understanding of change. More precise knowledge comes with absolute dating.

Absolute dating: King-lists and regnal years

Over a long period of time different dating systems came into existence. It is necessary to go a long way back into human history to discover how human beings learned to measure time in absolute dates. Men and women in all societies seem to have needed to know when an event occurred as well as where. No dating is possible without a point in time from which dates can be measured, a beginning. The simplest and nearest to everyone was birth; in a special way Christian dating begins from birth, the incarnation of Christ. But long before the Christian calendar was thought of the three score years and ten of a human life was a convenient measure of the passage of time. As with many later starting points there could be confusion because while most societies assumed that a new born infant had no age, so was 0, some societies, the Chinese for example, believe that a baby is 1 when born. Counting the passage of time in successive lives, or generations, was a logical next step. A generation, 'the average time in which children are ready to take the place of their parents', as the *Concise Oxford Dictionary* defines it, has become standardised, 'usually reckoned at about 30 years'.

For wider acceptance of a common dating system a well known, prominent person's life was used, most commonly the local ruler. King-lists took the place of generations. These lists of successive rulers with the period of time for which each person ruled, *not the length of their lives*, are first recorded in Sumer, Mesopotamia in about 2000 BC. Events were recorded as having taken place in the Xth year of a particular ruler. The books of the Old Testament record events in this way. 1 Kings 14 tells us that: 'In Judah Rehoboam son of Solomon had become king ... he reigned for seventeen years ... He was succeeded by his son Abijam [who] reigned for three years', and so on. What is significant is that the major events – in the main religious ones – are recorded in the context of kings' reigns. Thus Manasseh 'did what was wrong in the eyes of the Lord, in following the abominable practices of the nations which the Lord had dispossessed in favour of the Israelites. He rebuilt the hill-shrines which his father Hezekiah had destroyed, he erected altars to the Baal' [2 Kings 21]. The ancient Egyptians grouped the reigns of their rulers, their pharaohs, by families known as dynasties ['lines of hereditary rulers' COD]. Traditional history teaching in British schools followed this most ancient pattern, setting events in the reigns of particular monarchs and dividing the past into dynastic periods, such as Tudor or Stuart.

The Romans dated events by the years in which particular consuls held office and later by the reigns of Caesars. 'In the fifteenth year of the Emperor Tiberius, when Pontius Pilate was governor of Judaea, when Herod was prince of Galilee ... the word of God came to John' [Luke 3.1]. One of the commonest ways of dating documents in the Middle Ages and later was by the year of the sovereign's reign. These are called *regnal years*; Appendix 1 explains how they were calculated. Other important individuals could also be used for dating: some medieval British institutions dated documents by the year in office of their heads. For example, documents from the royal chancery may be dated by the chancellor's years in office. The names of bishops and of abbots may be used in the same way in dating ecclesiastical and manorial documents. Documents originating in Rome often used papal years. Appendix 2 explains how these dates can be discovered. Another method commonly used in medieval documents of any kind, to fix dates within the year, is by reference to religious festivals and saints' days. The explanation of these will be made later [see p 21] in connection with the Christian year.

Universal systems

All dating by the name of an individual, saint, king, pope or chancellor, has a defect: their dates are only recognised within the particular society in which the named person exercised authority. For records which covered more than one community a more widely accepted starting date, from which the passage of time could be calculated, was needed. The Neo-Babylonian Empire calculated time from what is in the Christian calendar 747 BC; it was the year of 'the accession of Nabonidus'. The independent Greek states adopted a 'fixed date by which all reckonings might be adjusted, the year when the record of Olympian victors began'; this was the victory of Coroebus in the Olympic footrace of 776 BC. The Romans calculated the passage of time from 'the Foundation of the City (753 BC)'.[9] It is interesting that the French revolutionaries for a short period used a new calendar based on a political event, the Revolution [see Appendix 3]. There was even a similar proposal, not put into practice, after the Russian Revolution of 1917. After the execution of Charles I the English Commonwealth government dated state documents from 1649, 'the first year of freedom', but it did not reform the calendar. The most widely used and longest lasting of imperial dating systems was the Chinese, which also spread to neighbouring countries [see Appendix 4]. These political systems had limitations; each was based on a geographically defined society. Wide as were the Roman and Chinese empires their dating systems did not survive. What did was that of the religion which superseded Rome; it had even replaced the Chinese system by the twentieth century [see p 24].

The only really lasting systems of universal dating have come from religions. The Jewish, Christian and Muslim religions have each produced dating systems in worldwide usage. Appendix 5 explains the Jewish calendar and Appendix 6 the Muslim calendar. The dating system which became most widely accepted was the Christian, which overwhelmed most local cultures between the sixteenth and twentieth centuries, as nominally Christian European countries conquered the bulk of the globe in a tide of imperial expansion.

Christian dating

There is no certain historical date for the birth of Jesus. The Gospel evidence is contradictory; Jesus was probably born in AD 4. However centuries later what was then the supposed year of Jesus Christ's 'incarnation' ['embodiment in human flesh' COD] was adopted as the beginning of the Christian era. This first and all following years are described as ANNO DOMINI [AD], in the year of Our Lord. The years before Christ's incarnation were counted backwards and, surprisingly in view of the use of Latin for AD, described in the vernacular: Before Christ [BC] in English, *Vor Christ* which means the same in German. There is no year 0; AD 1 follows 1 BC.

Such Christian dating has long been used in Europe and the Americas but it has been increasingly recognised that this is based on an event of major significance only to Christians. The introduction of radiocarbon dating led to an attempt to develop a system without religious overtones, which could be accepted by Muslims and other non-Christians. This was based on 1950, the year radiocarbon dating was discovered; BP (Before the Present) was to be used for dates before 1950. It has proved only partially acceptable and is only generally used when dealing with dates which are many thousands of years ago. There is a further complication: some German archaeologists use the very similar *Vor unser Zeit* (before our time) for BC dates.

The first use of Christ's incarnation in a time series was by a monk, Dionysius Exiguus, in AD 525, when compiling a table to calculate the changing dates of Easter. In the mid-7th century Wilfred persuaded the English church to adopt the Roman way of calculating the date of Easter, and so to adopt Dionysius' table and chronology. Dionysius' 'device was adopted for chronological purposes by Bede [and] starting from English usage in the eighth century, [observance of] the new era gradually spread to the Continent until in every country of Western Europe except Spain Christians reckoned from AD 1' [Cheney p.1]. In Spain and Portugal the Christian era began in 38 BC, because the Visigoths had adopted an earlier Easter Table, used by the Christians in Roman Spain, which was calculated from 38 BC. This usage was given up at different dates in the separate Iberian kingdoms between 1180 (Catalonia) and 1420 (Portugal).

Easter and the Christian calendar

Calendars are systems for recording the beginning and end of the year with fixed subdivisions. The Christian calendar is not simple because, while most annually recurring events are always on the same day of the year, others move [see Appendix 7]. The moveable feast of Easter is the key to such changes in both the Roman and the Orthodox calendars. The changes in the date of Easter were laid down by the Council of Nicaea in AD 325. Britain adopted the Roman dating for Easter at the Synod of Whitby in AD 663.[10] When Easter should be celebrated in each year was a matter of dispute between Christian churches. The final Roman decision was that it 'should be celebrated on the Sunday following the first full moon on or after the 21 March' [Cheney p7].

The 21 March was taken to be invariably the date of the Spring equinox, which it was not. This was a development from the complex decision of the Council of Nicaea and led to different ways of calculating Easter in the Roman and Greek churches [see Appendix 8]. The earliest possible date for Easter is 22 March, the latest 25 April.

Thirty-six Tables 'for all possible dates of Easter' in the Roman usage are in Cheney [pp 84-155].[11] To discover which of these tables applies to any particular year the student has to know when Easter was in that year. Cheney's 'Chronological Table of Easter Days' from AD 500 to AD 2000 [pp 156-61] provides answers, as do his Tables of 'Regnal Years' [see footnote on p 18]. The differences in the Orthodox calendar are explained in Appendix 6. Caution is necessary in using Cheney's tables of Easter dates. They are based on the modern (Roman) calendar year beginning on 1 January but *in England the year began on 25 March until 1752* [see pp 22]. So for dates between 1 January and 24 March before 1752 great care has to be taken, because they may well relate to what would, in today's notation, be the following year. The diagram on p. 25 may help to make this clear.

Leap years [see p 24] are one problem. The first two columns of Cheney's Easter tables list the dates and days in January and February in leap years, when an extra day is fitted in before Easter. In the Roman calendar February 1492 was a leap year, with 29 days, but to the English church in the Middle Ages this was February 1491 because the English New Year then began on 25 March [see p 22]. Moveable feasts in the early part of the year need careful checking. An English medieval date such as the Wednesday after Epiphany 1481 should not be looked for in Cheney's Table 32, for 1481, but in Table 17 for 1482, since Epiphany comes in January. The worst difficulty comes in dating a moveable feast which in different years may be before or after 24/25 March; the alternatives have to be checked. This is not helped when the document has used the year beginning on 1 January instead of 25 March, which does occasionally happen in the late Middle Ages. For example, in what year was a document bearing the date 'the Thursday before Palm Sunday 1472' actually written and dated? If Palm Sunday in Cheney's tables was before 25 March, this should be 1473 in our dating, but if Palm Sunday was after 25 March the document should be from 1472. Palm Sunday in 1472 was on March 22 [Cheney Table 8 p 98]; in 1473 on 11 April [Cheney Table 28 p 138]. This means that the document cannot have been dated using a year beginning on 25 March. 1 January must have been used; so the year given in the document, 1472, is the year in our modern dating. Wills may use the modern dating while the probate date in the church court may not, which could well make it appear that the will was proved before it was made!

Saints' days and religious festivals

As has been mentioned [p 18] the use of religious festivals and saints' days to date medieval documents is common. To turn these into modern dating is a little complicated but with the help of Cheney usually quite manageable. For example, the date 'the Wednesday after the feast of St Martin the Bishop, 8 Henry V' is 13 November 1420. To calculate this the student needs first to discover what year was 8 Henry V (the 8th year of the reign of Henry V, dated from the day after his accession day). Cheney's list of the 'Rulers of England' [pp 18-31] reveals that this was 21 March 1420 to 20 March 1421. There is in Cheney [pp 43-64] a list of 'Saints' Days and Festivals used in Dating'. There are two *'Martinus'* in this; the one which we want will be *'Martinus ep'* [*episcopus* = bishop]. He has two feast days: 11 November, the day of his death or martyrdom, and 4 July, the date of his 'ordination and translation', that is of his consecration and of the movement of his relics. There must have been a coincidence in the day of the year. Since there is no mention of ordination or translation in the document we can assume that 11 November is meant. This must therefore be 11 November 1420. Cheney's Table for Easter 1420 [pp 116-7] shows that the Wednesday after 11 November was 13 November.

There are some sources of confusion in identifying the correct saint. Some names are common to more than one saint, as in the case of Martin, John, Mary and Thomas. Cheney's introduction to his 'Saints' Days' list [pp 40-42] should be read carefully. He gives a fascinating example of how confusion between two Thomases was unravelled. Sometimes the local celebration may be confusing. Norwich Cathedral, for example, is dedicated to Holy Trinity and celebrates its feast on 24 September, but Trinity Sunday is a moveable feast, fifty-seven days after Easter, NOT 24 September.

Many church festivals are 'moveable feasts' dependent on the date of Easter in any particular year. For example, Ascension is on the Thursday after Rogation Sunday which itself was on the thirty-sixth day after Easter [see Appendix 7]. So to date a document in which Ascension is used as a reference point the date of Easter in the year of the document has first to be discovered, in the way which has already been described [p 20]. A list of medieval holy days is in Appendix 9.[12]

It was common practice in the middle ages to write of the *octave* in connection with festivals. The octave was the seventh day after a festival. The word could also be used to describe the period of eight days which included the festival and its octave day.

3

THE YEAR AND ITS DIVISIONS

The year[13] began at different times in different calendars. The Muslim New Year, 1 Muharram, was on 9 May in 1997 [see Appendix 6]. The Jewish New Year, 1 Tishri, is on different dates each year [see Appendix 5], as is the Chinese year. The *Independent*, on 20 March 1996, published the following item in explanation of Omar Khayyam's poem, *Norooz*, which begins:

'The New Year breeze is sweet upon the rose's cheek'.

'Today is the Spring Equinox, when the sun crosses the earth's equator ... It is also the Persian New Year. From time immemorial Zoroastrians celebrated the end of winter and the arrival of a new season of fertility and abundance. They called it Norooz, which means "the new day" and it survived into the Islamic period as a festival and annual commemoration of Jamshid, the most famous mythical Persian king and inventor of wine. Persian poets have always evoked Norooz as a symbol of hope and renewal, a time when old sorrows are forgotten and love blossoms, when nature's resurrection is reflected in the human heart and soul'.[14]

To begin the New Year with 'nature's resurrection' is entirely logical, and 25 March, the medieval church's chosen date, was in this respect most appropriate. While the acceptance of Christ's incarnation as the beginning of the Christian era became universal in Europe, the day on which the year started was not generally agreed until the twentieth century. Cheney has three pages [pp 4-6] describing the European variants. Dorothy Whitelock explains the 'different styles of beginning the year' which made the dates given in the different manuscripts of the Anglo-Saxon Chronicle so confusing [see p 14]: the year '794 begins at Christmas ... there is no clear indication of any other usage until 851, which begins in the autumn, presumably on 24 September with the Caesarean Indication.* ... A reversion to Christmas dating for 891-896 has been suggested ... in the eleventh century another method competed with Christmas, dating from the Annunciation on 25 March.'[15] 1 January was the beginning of the Roman year and this usage survived through the Middle Ages, but the Church preferred to start the year on a major Christian festival. The feast of the Annunciation of the Blessed Virgin Mary (BVM) or Lady Day, 25 March, became the most commonly accepted first day of the year. By the twelfth century this was the norm in England and it lasted until 1752.

On 24 February 1582 Pope Gregory XIII introduced major changes to the Christian calendar. The solar and calendar year had diverged since Julius Caesar had instituted the Roman calendar in 45 BC. The Roman calendar year

* For 'Indiction' see Cheney pp 2-3

7. Pope Gregory XIII (a 16th century bust in the Museo Civico in Bologna): the reform of the calendar under Gregory XIII in 1586 provided the basis for the system of measuring time which has lasted to the present day, although for religious reasons it was not adopted in Protestant countries of northern Europe until the 18th century.

had contained 365 days with every fourth year containing an extra day. This calculation of 365¼ days in the year slightly overestimated the actual length of the solar year. The calendar year became too long. So the Pope dropped ten days, the excess of days which had accumulated in the intervening 1627 years, ordering that 4 October 1582 should be followed by 15 October. To prevent the same error occurring in the future the Pope ordered that from 1600 only one in every four of the end years of centuries were to be 'leap' years, but neither 2000 nor 4000 were to be leap years, to adjust for a slight over-correction. From 1583 the year was to start on 1 January.[16]

Because of the bitter religious divisions of sixteenth century Europe, the 'New Style' Gregorian calendar was not universally adopted. Protestant and Orthodox countries continued to use the 'Old Style' Julian calendar. The years in which different countries adopted the New Style Calendar were:

1582	Italy	France	Spain	Portugal	
1583	Prussia	Switzerland	Holland	Flanders	Catholic states in Germany
1586	Poland				
1587	Hungary				
1600	Scotland adopted 1 January as the beginning of the year but not the Gregorian calendar					
1700	Protestant states in Germany Denmark					
1700-40	Sweden, by omission of 11 leap years					
1752	All of Britain adopted the Gregorian calendar and England, Ireland & Wales began the year on 1 January					
1872	Japan				
1912	China				
1915	Bulgaria				
1917	Turkey USSR				
1919	Yugoslavia Romania					
1923	Greece				

It is not difficult to imagine the confusion which arose with countries starting the year on different days and being ten or more days apart in their dating. Historical students have to be extremely careful in interpreting the dates on documents after 1582; there were so many different practices in European countries. While Scotland, from 1600, began the year on 1 January, England did not officially do so until 1752. We describe Charles I's execution as having taken place on 30 January 1649, but to English contemporaries it was 30 January 1648. Dates between 1 January and 25 March were commonly written, as Charles I's execution might have been, 164⁸⁄₉.

However, to complicate matters still further, the official system was not used for everyday purposes. The January to December year was always regarded, for *most* everyday purposes, as the relevant one. It was the farmer's year.

Seventeenth and eighteenth century cookery books use this calendar year in their charts of how to plan the gathering of the preservation of food. '1 January was regarded as New Year's Day by diarists and almanac makers, and also marked the start of the liturgical year'.[17]

Pepys described 1 January as New Year's Day in his diary, but began each year on 25 March. Some English journals in the early eighteenth century began their volume years in January. The biggest confusion, however, arose over the difference in dates between countries using the Old and the New Styles. To avoid this confusion a system of double dating was adopted, particularly in foreign correspondence. John Churchill wrote his famous note to his wife Sarah announcing his victory at Blenheim, dating it 13 August 1704, the date of the battle in European style. His aide-de-camp delivered the note to Sarah on 10 August, English style. This would have been written as $\frac{10}{21}$ August, which combined the English date (10th) and the European one (21st), so avoiding any confusion.

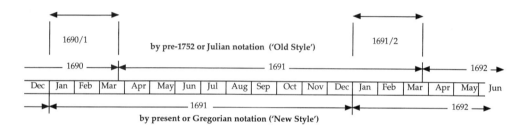

8. Diagram to illustrate the relationship between the 'Old Style' and 'New Style' calendars.

Britain abandoned the Julian and adopted the Gregorian calendar in 1752. As a result of Chesterfield's Act, of March 1751, the year 1752 began on 1 January, and 2 September was followed by 14 September. While the 'give us back our eleven days riots' often noted in historical writing have been shown in a fascinating article to have been at least much exaggerated, there is widespread evidence for a longlasting acceptance of the old calendar in practice. Almanac makers continued, in many cases, to print both the old and new dates. Old Christmas Day was only the most popular of many Old Style festivals which continued to be commemorated. 'As late as 1879, Shaw Wakes near Oldham was remembered as taking place "first Saturday after Old Lammas Day"'. Agricultural activities and, for example, fairs followed the natural year, changing their dates. Legal activities moved with the New Style. Poole has summed up the effect of the introduction of the New Style: it was 'a separation not only of two calendars but of two cultures. The cycle of popular festivities, the plebeian festive calendar, was left wedded to the agricultural year and to local circumstances, and separated from that of the church, state and polite urban society'.[18]

One British institution has, to this day, failed to adjust. Britain is unique in beginning its official financial year on 5 April. Until 1752 the first day of the year *and* the last day of the financial quarter was 25 March. The adjustment to the Gregorian calendar added eleven days, so 25 March became 5 April, and the last day of the financial year. The Treasury adjusted the days but unlike government institutions in the majority of countries, it could not adjust its workings to begin the financial year on 1 January. One of the more confusing anniversaries which adjustments to the calendar have produced is that of the Russian 'October' Revolution which was celebrated on 7 November. The Bolshevik revolution in Czarist Russia took place on 26 October 1917, Old Style. The new rulers of what became the USSR adopted the New Style; so 26 October became 7 November. The citizens of the Soviet Union 'lost' twelve days.

9. The Oxfordshire Election of 1754: one of the issues in this election, which produced some rioting, was the recent passing of the 1752 Act whereby the Gregorian Calendar was adopted throughout the United Kingdom. In the foreground a 'bludgeon man' is having his wounds dressed and under his foot is a captured banner reading GIVE US OUR ELEVEN DAYS.

The month

The ancient Roman year, from which the Christian months came, began in March and had ten months. January and February were soon added. The Roman months are listed in Appendix 10. Since they were all lunar months the year was too short. The pontiffs (*Pontifex Maximus*, the high priest), who were responsible for making adjustments to the calendar, were neglectful, so that the civil year fell behind the astronomical year. By the time that Julius Caesar reformed the calendar in 45 BC there was an error of three months between the civil equinox of 21 March and the astronomical equinox. Julius Caesar introduced an extra day in every fourth ('leap') year, to prevent the disparity between the calendar and astronomical year recurring but, as we have seen, over ensuing centuries the small annual differences became, cumulatively, a large discrepancy. The Roman calendar was largely used by Church authorities through the middle ages, but it was rivalled by dating by the feasts of the Church and numbering the days of the month as today. Medieval writers were slapdash in their use of the Roman calendar, as explained by Cheney who has printed the Roman and Christian calendars in parallel [pp 75-81].

The week

The week is an entirely artificial unit for which many explanations have been produced. While the Jewish and Christian week, and some others, have seven days, in Africa, for instance, there have been longer weeks. The names of the days of the week began in Latin, from which the French names are derived, but the English use Germanic/Scandinavian equivalents, except for Saturday; in part, the Germans do the same.

Latin	French	English	German
Dies Solis [Sun]	Dimanche	Sunday [Sun]	Sonntag
Dies Lunae [Moon]	Lundi	Monday [Moon]	Montag
Dies Martis [Mars]	Mardi	Tuesday [Tiw=Mars]	Dienstag [Service Day]
Dies Mercurius [Mercury]	Mercredi	Wednesday [Woden/Odin]	Mittwoch [Mid-week]
Dies Jovis [Jove]	Jeudi	Thursday [Thor/Thunder]	Donnerstag [Thunder]
Dies Veneris [Venus]	Vendredi	Friday [Frigg, Odin's wife]	Freitag
Dies Saturni [Saturn]	Samedi	Saturday [Saturn]	Samstag

10. A scale copy of the dials of the highly-elaborate astronomical clock which was constructed for Hampton Court Palace in 1540; the dials have epicyclic gearing and give moon and calendar indications with zodiacal symbols to cover the full year.

11. Lantern clock with anchor escapement, made by John Drury in about 1700: as clocks became a familiar household item, the opportunities for decorative work and beautiful brass and other ornamentation were soon realised, so that they became attractive ornaments as well as functional items.

Some countries, such as Greece, simply give the days of the week numbers: Monday is DEUTERA, Tuesday TRITE, and so on. The Quakers (Society of Friends) do the same, numbering the days of the week. For Quaker dating see Appendix 11.

The day

A twenty-four hour day has been in use almost from time immemorial, but the beginning of the day has varied. 'Dawn was used by the ancient Egyptians, whereas sunset was chosen by the Babylonians, Jews and Muslims. The Romans at first chose sunrise but later midnight. Dawn was the beginning of the day unit in Western Europe before the advent of the striking clock in the fourteenth century. Astronomers found it more convenient to choose midday, and this remained the beginning of the astronomical day until 1 January 1925 when, by international agreement, the astronomical day was made to coincide with the civil day'.[19] The same practice was followed 'in ships' log-books from the seventeenth century until early in the nineteenth' [Cheney p 10]. The day's date, therefore, began at midday. Trafalgar, fought in the afternoon of 21 October, is recorded in the *Victory's* log-book under 22 October 1805. The Jewish day starts everywhere at sunset, whatever clock time that may be. So the Sabbath starts at different times in England and Israel, indeed in Cardiff and London. For religious purposes the day is taken as beginning fifteen minutes earlier than sunset, as a safeguard against breaking a Sabbath rule by accident.

The time at any given place on the earth is measured according to when the sun is directly over that place. This is midday, twelve o'clock. Since the earth rotates on its axis time varies depending on where a place is. All holiday makers going abroad are well aware of this. How far time in a particular place is ahead of or behind British time, which is Greenwich Mean Time, depends on how many degrees longitude separate the place from Greenwich which is on Longitude 0°. Greenwich Mean Time is calculated from when the sun is directly over Greenwich; this is 12.00 midday. At the International Dateline, on Longitude 180°, the day starts at midnight. Countries to the east of this line are a day ahead of those to the west.[20] There was no standard British time until the nineteenth century. 'In the late eighteenth century, stage coaches travelling east and west observed local time, carrying with them clocks set to gain or lose in conformity with the migrating sun'.[21] The Determination of Time Act of 1880 gave legal force to the use of a national standard time which the spread of railways had necessitated.

12. The Greenwich Meridian, with the Old Observatory in the background: the Greenwich Meridian was established as the line of longitude from which all international time is measured.

4
THE COMING OF MODERN TIME-KEEPING

In pre-modern society customary measurement of the passage of time during the day was not by hourly divisions. Before clocks were commonly available the passage of time was measured by light and dark. The working day was longer in the summer than in the winter. Sundials and scratch dials were used; some examples of scratch dials on church towers have the time of service more deeply indented. On the window sill of farm houses and cottages a mark was sometimes made, which recorded the midday sun so that the wife could summon the men to a meal. J. M. Synge described how the knowledge of time on the Aran islands depended 'upon the direction of the wind. If the wind is northerly the south door is opened, and the shadow of the door-post moving across the kitchen floor indicates the hour'. When the wind changed and the north door was opened, 'the people, who never think of putting up a primitive dial, are at a loss'.[22]

13. Plaster cast of an Egyptian shadow clock, made in green schist (10th-8th centuries BC): it was placed on an east-west alignment so that the morning sun threw a shadow of the upturned end onto the base, and at noon the position of the clock was reversed.

14. Plaster cast of a Saxon sundial on the church at Kirkdale, Yorkshire: sundials were a familiar feature of many church or churchyard walls for centuries.

15. French column sundial, 17th century: this sundial has been calibrated for use at about 45° north. It is set up for use in a particular month (thereby allowing for the changes in the relative position of the earth and the sun) by rotating the dragon until its tail is immediately above the appropriate sign of the zodiac shown in relief at the base of the column. The whole sundial is then rotated until the shadow of the dragon's tail lies in a vertical line down the side of the column. The time is read off from the position of the shadow of the tip of the tail. When time is found from the sun's altitude in this way the same reading will be given for, say, 10am and 2pm and readings around noon will be imprecise as the sun's altitude is changing slowly.

16. A French universal ring sundial: made of brass and partly-silvered, it indicates time by light from the sun passing through a pinhole onto a graduated ring parallel to the earth's equator.

In this traditional world church bells could be used to mark outstanding events in the year and even important times on special days, such as the beginning of gleaning. There was an audible measure of the passage of time for those near a church. The first clocks in English cathedrals appeared in the late thirteenth century. Significantly they usually contained astronomical information and measured the cycle of the year. Landes argues that mechanical clocks were invented in Europe, rather than in China which had far more advanced water clocks, because of the monastic need to keep the hours of the day and night accurately. 'This religious concern for punctuality may seem foolish to rationalists of the twentieth century, but it was no small matter to a monk of the Middle Ages'.[23] To this was added the need of an urban bourgeoisie for a measurement of time more regular than the natural divisions of the day which served the peasant.

'The introduction of equal hours and the habituation of urban populations to public time announcements had profound consequences. Medieval man was innumerate as well as illiterate. Units of distance were linked to physical characteristics that varied as people do (the English *foot*, for instance). All this began to change in the twelfth and thirteenth centuries. It was no accident that Arabic numerals came in at this time.'[23] 'From the fourteenth century onwards church clocks and public clocks were erected in the cities and large market towns of England. The majority of English parishes must have possessed church clocks by the end of the sixteenth century'.[24] They were usually in visually dominant towers, and widely resounding. Those in sight of a clock could see the time. Those further afield could hear the hours striking.

Landes has described in technical detail how timers developed bells and how the new escapement and falling weights made the mechanical clock possible. 'The mechanical clock began as a crude, imprecise, unreliable instrument. It took four hundred years to turn it into an accurate timepiece'.[25] Domestic longcase and grandfather clocks spread in England from the end of the seventeenth century, becoming widespread in better off houses during the eighteenth century. Francis Steer has described the spread of clocks in Essex: 'Our first reference to a clock is in 1670; the next is in 1679. From that date clocks become more frequent, but are never described in much detail ... after the Restoration, the production of weight- and spring-driven clocks rapidly increased in England. At the same time, the Dutch invention of the pendulum was developed, and long-case rather than wall clocks were made in this country. From about 1690 we have references to clocks and cases, which are listed simply as 'a clock and weights'. Even with the growing popularity of clocks towards the end of the seventeenth century hour-glasses did not go out of fashion'.[26] It should be remembered that these inventories are of dead people's possessions; so the clocks were probably *bought* much earlier than the date of the inventory. Steer's earliest five inventories, from between 1670 and

17. Longcase clock, made by Thomas Tompion circa 1700: longcase clocks of this type were made in ever-increasing numbers after pendulums were applied to clockwork mechanisms in the mid-17th century. By the middle of the 18th century most towns had a clockmaker and some, such as Prescot in Lancashire, had developed a specialised industry manufacturing the delicate and often very small parts required for clocks and watches. By that time, too, a 'grandfather' clock was a typical item of furniture in many thousands of middle class and yeoman households.

1696, are those of a gentleman, three yeomen, and a miller.

Industrialisation led to a much greater need to measure time more precisely and for ordinary working people to have access to measures of time. Factories worked to fixed hours and needed a workforce which could be relied on to come to work on time. Railways had timetables. The clock at Bristol Temple Meads station was set on local time, ten minutes different from Greenwich time. This put the timetable out, so Bristol and London time had to be standardised. The guards on trains from London carried watches set on London time from which the clocks on the stations to Bristol were regularly checked. Time was not standardised everywhere. Services in Christ Church Cathedral, Oxford still start on Oxford time. The 6pm service begins at 6.05. Milward and Saul comment that there was a much 'greater need of people to have a watch in the 1840s with the introduction of railway timetables and the spread of more regular working hours'. So the Swiss watchmaking industry was transformed. By '1872 366,000 watches and watch movements were exported to the United States alone'.[27]

18. Charing Cross railway station in the 1870s: railway station clocks had a profound influence upon the lives of ordinary people, for it was the need for timetables and standardised time (without which no railway could operate) which produced the concept of a national time to supersede the innumerable local variations of time which had functioned for many centuries.

Before there were cheap enough watches or clocks for all to buy, or universal public clocks, the 'knocker-up' emerged in the industrial areas of northern Britain. He was a man, with a timepiece which woke him, who went round the workers' houses with a long stick knocking on the upstairs bedroom windows. A north country folk-tale, 'Never come Monday', satirises the change in lifestyle from living by the external cycle of nature to becoming dependent on a mechanical device. The knocker-up's clock stopped one Monday; so there was no knocking-up and everyone slept on, believing it was Sunday!

19. The 'knocker-up' was a familiar figure – at least to early risers – on the streets of many northern industrial towns until the 1950s. This evocative photograph was taken in 1960 and shows Hiram Taylor, aged 82 years, just before his retirement from the job of 'knocker-up' at Oswaldtwistle, Lancashire. The rain-washed setts and terraced houses are in Worsley Street, Oswaldtwistle, and this, like the knocker-up and his way of life, is now vanished for ever. Digital radio alarm clocks have superseded the job and redeveloped housing has replaced the street where he lived.

5

DATING IN OTHER CONTEXTS

Dating letters

Cheney's calendars have a use which is not explained, perhaps because it is too obvious; family historians in particular, but not only they, can use the Easter Tables in a special way. Many students will have come across letters, most often Victorian but of other periods too, which while voluminous and informative will, maddeningly, be inadequately dated. If by any lucky chance the envelope survives the post mark will solve the problem. More often one has to make use of what evidence the writer has left by way of dating. If an approximate date, within seven years, is known, Cheney's Easter Tables can provide answers. If the day and the date of the month are given the year can be discovered. Sometimes only the date of the month may be in the heading but the day can be worked out from the contents. Conversely if one knows the year and date of the month the day can be established. This amount of detail may not seem to matter very much, but the understanding of a continuing correspondence may depend on knowing the order of the letters and the intervals between them.

Examples may make this clearer. I have a group of letters written between 1860 and 1884 by my great-great-grandmother, Margaret Copeland. They are dated in many different ways, but I have been able to date them precisely and to arrange them in the order in which they were written, using Cheney's Easter Tables. A letter headed 'Friday 12 February' must have been written in 1869 or 1875 [Cheney's Table 7]. From the content it must have been from 1869. Another letter dated 'Nov 2nd' was in an envelope with the postmark 'No 2 71'. November 2nd 1871 was a Thursday [Cheney's Table 19]. A third letter has only the date '9 Dec', but it contains a warning to her daughter who lived in Eyam against witnessing 'the Doings at Chatsworth' because of the weather, followed by a reference to the Prince. It should be possible to discover from biographies and local newspapers when the Prince of Wales was at Chatsworth and which of several visits was in a year that was appropriate for the correspondence. As it happens Margaret Copeland's granddaughter noted in her diary for 1872 under 18 and 21 December that she went to Chatsworth and saw the Prince and Princess. Her grandmother's letter must have been written on Monday 9 December 1872 [Cheney's Table 10], which date fits in quite appropriately in the sequence of letters. In later life, incidentally, Margaret Copeland often dated her letters fully, eg 'Roselands in Bed 12 o'clock Friday 21 February 1879'!

The researcher cannot, however, assume infallibility in Victorian dating by letter writers. The diary writer, my grandmother, wrote over 100 letters to my grandfather between January and June 1883 almost all dated accurately in various ways. However 'Sunday Evening May 18 1883' is followed after a letter dated 'May 19' by one headed 'Trinity Sunday May 20 1883'. This last one was accurate. The earlier mistake is particularly surprising because the writer was a rector's daughter living in a rectory and a great Sunday churchgoer. It was good advice that my grandmother's older brother had given his mother in a letter from Switzerland of 'Tuesday March 3d/74'. 'Put the day of the week as well as the day of the month on your letter as I do, it makes them so much more understandable'. In some early sixteenth century correspondence the same advice is given but *not* practised by the writer. Hugh Parker, a Lancashire gentleman, wrote from Peel, Isle of Man, to his brother George, who was looking after Hugh's estates while he was absent: 'I praye you to make me no more bylles bot set the day of the mone & in qwat yere of the Rene of the Kynge'. The letter was dated 'xviijd of aprylys' *without* any year. Not one of the letters Hugh wrote is adequately dated![28] Anyone who has experienced the frustration of having to arrange a badly dated correspondence in chronological order will appreciate the need to follow such advice. It applies to many other historical 'documents': dating photographs is particularly important. Much invaluable information has been lost because the photographer who 'knows' when the photograph was taken forgets that others, who may want to use the evidence in it, DON'T.

Institutional records[29]

The law courts and the older universities in England, Oxford and Cambridge, divide their years into 'terms', while Parliament has 'sessions'. The law courts have four terms in a year, the universities three, and they do not always use the same name for the parallel term. The calendar year begins with a *Hilary* term in the law courts and Oxford, but with a *Lent* term in Cambridge. Oxford follows with a *Trinity* term, the law courts and Cambridge with an *Easter* term; these usually begin in April. The extra law courts' term, *Trinity*, is in July, when the universities are on vacation. The University (academic) year begins in October with a *Michaelmas* term. The last law term of the calendar year, also *Michaelmas*, began in October but was moved to later dates in the seventeenth and eighteenth centuries, and from 1831 to November.

Cheney explains the extremely complicated dates of the medieval law terms [pp 65-69]. 'Certain days and seasons [were] excluded [religious feasts and] periods during which the Church had forbidden certain types of oath to be taken. The third excluded season was due to the harvest and fear of the plague during the hot season in town' [pp 65-66]. Law terms always begin on a Monday and end on a Thursday. Appendix 12 is a calendar of institutional dates. As their name implies local quarter sessions met four times a year, at Easter, Trinity, Michaelmas and Epiphany. The actual days on which the magistrates met have been different in different jurisdictions and in different years.

Parliament's business was and is divided into 'sessions' which Cheney describes as 'the chronological and procedural unit of parliamentary business' [p. 70]. They have been of different lengths at different periods in the past. Parliamentary sessions nowadays last from September or October in one year until September or October of the following year, with an adjournment between July and October. Statutes of the realm are identified in relation to the session in which they become law. There are informative essays about parliament in Powicke and Fryde[30] and in Cheney [p. 70-72]. The dating of modern statutes is explained in Butler: 'the act listed as 11 & 12 Geo VI c.65 was the [sixty-fifth Act] passed in the parliamentary session during the eleventh and twelfth regnal years of George VI',[31] which were 11 December 1946 to 10 December 1947 and 11 December 1947 to 10 December 1948. So 11 & 12 Geo VI c.65 was passed between September/October 1947 and July 1948. In the text of the Act it was dated 30 July 1948, so it became law only just before the session ended.

The ritual year

The institutional calendar reflected a different culture to that of 'the plebian festival calendar'.[32] The peasant's daily round was measured by natural phenomena. Phythian Adams, in a pioneering work, pointed out that 'even after the fourteenth century when some churches were beginning to boast clocks, the days—and hence the hours—varied in their length from winter to summer according to the light'.[33] 'The village calendar moved with the seasons'.[34] The farming calendar was interwoven with pagan and Christian feasts to form what has come to be called the Ritual Year. Customary festivals, some pre-Christian, others relatively modern such as Oak-apple Day and Guy Fawkes, became in time linked with the Church. St Bride's or St Bridget's day, 1 February, is a christianisation of a pagan goddess, 'a provider of plenty and a friend of animals, with a very close association with the whole natural world'.[35] On Oak-apple Day, 29 May, oak galls or oak branches were worn by people; then oak boughs came to be put on church towers. On Guy Fawkes Day, 5 November, bonfires were lit universally and in some churches the bells were rung; 'the winter-season ringing of the church bells used to commence on the 5th of November'.[36]

Both these two festivals were entirely secular in origin. The study of the complex interweaving of different elements in the Ritual Year has occupied generations of folklorists and historians from Brand, Hone and Wright to Ronald Hutton [see Bibliography]. Phythian Adams has a calendar of some of the popular customs which can be supplemented from any or all of these four books.

20. 'Planting the village maypole' and 'The country maypole':
maypole ceremonies and dancing were found in many places. In
the 19th century the very obvious overtones of pagan or non-
Christian observance in events such as this (including all-too-
apparent sexual connotations and fertility symbols) together with
the 'unruliness and unseemliness of the behaviour of the crowd'
meant that local clergy frequently campaigned for their abolition
and replacement by more wholesome and virtuous festivals.

The association of so many of the dates in this calendar with the produce of woods and fields and water only underlines its closeness to the natural world. The *Twelve Days of Christmas* saw orgies of eating and drinking; there was a high birth rate nine months later. On Twelfth Night [Old Christmas Day] there was wassailing [drinking the health of] apple trees. St Agnes, 21 January, is symbolised by a snow-white lamb. St Bride, 1 February, was welcomed with rushes. Collops, slices of fried bacon and eggs, were eaten on Shrove Monday, pancakes on Shrove Tuesday when cock-throwing and cock-fighting were popular. St David's Day, 1 March, was celebrated by the Welsh with leeks. On Mothering Sunday there was a meal of loin of veal or hind quarter of lamb and consumption of the simnel cake. Carling, or Passion, Sunday was the day for eating peas (carlings) fried in butter. On Palm Sunday willow branches were gathered. On St Patrick's Day, 17 March, the Irish wore shamrocks. Good Friday is associated with hot cross buns and Easter Sunday with eggs. May Day saw the young collecting foliage, making garlands and bringing home the maypole. The next day, 2 May, was Rowantree or Witch Day on which rowan or mountain ash was collected to protect people from witches. Oak leaves were connected with 29 May because Charles II hid in an oak tree to escape capture. Sheep-shearing in June was celebrated with a dinner at which cheese cakes were customary. Strewing churches with rushes took place in July. St Swithin's Day, 15 July, was ominous for rain; it was the day for christening apples. On Lammas Day, 1 August, arable common fields were thrown open for pasture. On Michaelmas Day, 29 September, a goose was eaten. On St Faith's Day, 6 October, in the north of England, a cake was baked jointly by three maidens. On All Saints' Day, 1 November, 'soul cakes' were given to relatives and friends; this led to the custom of begging from door to door. St Clement's Day, 23 November, and St Catherine's Day, 25 November, were also occasions for door to door begging.

'Catherine and Clement come year by year,
Some of your apples and some of your beer'[37]

Christmas Eve and Christmas Day began the revelry which lasted for twelve days.

Many crafts had patron saints and their festival days were occasions for the craft to relax and indulge itself. St Distaff's [Rock] Day, 7 January, was the day on which women recommenced spinning. Plough Monday, in the second week of January—a secular festival—marked the return of men to field work. St Blaise's Day, 3 February, was the woolcombers' and weavers' day; St Piran's Day, 5 March, was the tin miners'; St Gregory's Day, 12 March, the farmers'; St Peter's Day, 29 June, was the fishermen's; St Crispin's Day, 25 October, the shoemakers'; St Clement's Day, 23 November, the blacksmiths'; and St Andrew's Day, 30 November, was the lacemakers' day. St Catherine, whose

21. First footing in 19th century Edinburgh: in Scotland 'first footers' were traditionally those who were the first to cross the threshold immediately after midnight on New Year's Day.

22. Plough Monday festivities: this romanticised view is taken from the Every Day Book of 1826. Such celebrations were widely held throughout England and Wales before the mid-19th century, though every community had its own local calendar and there were countless regional and local variations upon the themes printed in national calendars and lists.

day was 25 November, was the patron saint of many crafts. Most were concerned with a wheel: wheelwrights and carpenters, rope-makers and lacemakers; spinners brought the association with spinsters and so with girl students.

There is a noticeable difference between the two halves of the year. Many more popular festivals were concentrated in the first half of the year, between the Nativity in December and the Ascension in June. Phythian Adams pointed out that this 'critical season of seed time and growth', the least busy time of the farming year, was 'associated as a whole with the birth, death, and resurrection of Christ. The complementary nature of church and popular observances [made this] the most conspicuous part of the year for ritual activity'.

In contrast 'the period between Midsummer and Christmas in general was so lacking in ritual and symbolic continuity that it may fittingly be described as "secular", marked more by recreation and games than by ritual. Autumn and early winter were more concerned with old age, death and the after-life'.[38] When Henry VIII limited the numbers of holy days which might be celebrated, all feasts between 1 July and 29 September, ie harvest time, were no longer to be kept as holy days. Work was to be lawful 'as upon any other workye day'. The excessive growth of holy days in the middle ages had become 'prejudiciall to the commonweale, by reason that it is occasion of moche sloth and ydleness and losse of man's fode many tymes [since men did not take] the opportunitie of good and serene wheather offered upon the same [holy days] in time of harvest'. Furthermore 'the feast of dedication of the church shall in all places throughout this realm be celebrate and kept on the fyrst Sonday of the moneth of Octobre forever'.[39] These changes were introduced in an Act of 1536 for the abrogation of certain holydays.

Henry VIII's legislation and a technological revolution, which began before it with the creation of mechanical clocks and has accelerated ever since, have fundamentally changed our perception of the world in which we live. Time, for a growing proportion of the world's population, is no longer measured by light and dark or by spring and autumn but by quartz clocks.[40] Astronomical measurements of time are checked by an atomic frequency standard. To understand our past, however, we need to study the great variety of ways in which mankind has slowly learnt to measure time and date events in it.

Appendix 1

THE REGNAL YEARS

For local and family historians it is essential to understand what are known as 'regnal years', the years of each English sovereign's reign, because so many of the documents which they need to study make use of the monarch's reign as a method of dating. For example, George Kettell of King's Langley in Hertfordshire set his hand and seal to his will 'the fifteenthe daye of Julye in the 33th yere of the raigne of oure soveraigne lady Elizabeth'. Elizabeth I came to the throne in 1558. Since, therefore, 1558 was the first year of the reign one would expect the thirty-third year to have been 1590, but George Kettell went on in his will to add 'in the yeare of oure lorde god' 1591.[41] George Kettell was counting years from the day of the queen's accession, not from the beginning of the calendar year. He was using the regnal year. Cheney explains the English regnal years [pp.12-13] and lists them [pp.18-31] and they are given in table form at the end of this appendix.

Since Henry VIII's death a new monarch's regnal year dating has begun on the day the sovereign legally acceded to the throne, which was the day on which the previous sovereign died or abdicated, and ended on the eve of the anniversary of the accession in the next year. However, the accession of monarchs has not always been calculated in this way. The earliest monarch for whom a generally accepted usage existed was Henry II. His regnal year was measured from the day of his coronation, which was 19 December 1154, although his predecessor, Stephen, had died earlier, on 25 October 1154. The coronation day was taken as the first day of the regnal year until the death of Henry III in 1277. Edward I's reign was held to have begun four days after the death of his father, Henry III, but in turn his son, Edward II, dated his reign from the day after his father's death in 1207. This became the usual, though not invariable, pattern from that time until the death of Henry VIII in 1547.

There were other complications. John was crowned on Ascension Day, and perhaps because the coronation was a religious ceremony John's regnal years did not begin on the actual anniversary of the coronation - the day of the month on which he was crowned - but on Ascension Day in each succeeding year. Since Ascension Day is a movable feast each of John's regnal years is therefore different. As a result in some years, such as 1201-2, 1203-4, 1206-7, 1209-10, 1212-13 and 1214-15, the same date appears twice in a single regnal year. In the case of Edward III, Henry IV, Edward IV and Richard III, who succeeded on the deposition of the previous monarchs, the date of death of the predecessor was not strictly relevant to the calculation. The Wars of the Roses produced another anomaly. On 29 September 1470, during his tenth regnal year, Edward IV fled from England and on 3 October 1470 Henry VI was released from captivity, to be recrowned on 13 October. So there are documents dated in the forty-ninth year of the reign of Henry VI, from 9 October 1470 onwards. This year ended on 11 April 1471, when Henry VI was recaptured by Edward IV. The table below, which shows how this worked in reality, will make this clear:

1 Sep 1459 - 31 Aug 1460	38 Henry VI	
1 Sep 1460 - 4 Mar 1461	39 Henry VI	[deposed on 4 March]
4 Mar 1461 - 3 Mar 1462	1 Edward IV	
4 Mar 1462 - 3 Mar 1463	2 Edward IV	
4 Mar 1470 - 29 Sep 1470	10 Edward IV	[fled country]
9 Oct 1470 - 11 Apr 1471	49 Henry VI	[assumes that he had reigned continuously; captured on 11 April]
11 Apr 1471 - 3 Mar 1472	11 Edward IV	[assumes no interruption in his rule]

Since the death of Henry VIII there have been other reigns and periods in which the dating has been irregular. Lady Jane Grey 'reigned' from 6 July 1553, the day of Edward VI's death, until 19 July when Mary I deposed her. While Mary began her first regnal year on 19 July, she counted future regnal years from Edward's death on 6 July and thus dismissed Jane's brief 'reign'. She married Philip of Spain on 25 July 1554 and they began their joint regnal years on the day of the wedding.

Charles I was executed on 30 January 1649. As England was now a republic, only the year of the lord was used to date documents until Charles II returned to England on 29 May 1660. Charles II began to reign on that day, but assumed for dating purposes that he had become king on the death of his father, so dated 30 January 1660 to 29 January 1661 as his twelfth regnal year. All his later regnal years began on 30 January. The next hiatus came with James II's flight from London on 11 December 1688. From 12 December until 13 February 1689 there was an 'Interregnum', a period of time with no legal monarch. The joint reign of William III and Mary II began on 13 February 1689 and ended on 27 December 1694 when Mary died. William then reigned alone until his death. So 13 February 1694 to 27 December 1694 was the sixth *joint* regnal year and 28 December 1694 to 12 February 1695 was in William III's sixth regnal year. There was a change in the calendar in 1752 [see p 25] and in September the New Style of dating was adopted with the loss of eleven days. George II's twenty-sixth regnal year ran from 11 June 1752 to 21 June 1753, to make it 365 days long. The succeeding regnal years therefore ran from 22 June instead of 11 June.

Regnal years are still used in a few formal documents, such as those appointing sheriffs and lord lieutenants. They were used in Britain to identify statues of the realm or acts of parliament until 1962 [see p 42].

HENRY II

Regnal
Year

1	19 Dec 1154-18 Dec 1155		19	19 Dec 1172-18 Dec 1173
2	19 Dec 1155-18 Dec 1156		20	19 Dec 1173-18 Dec 1174
3	19 Dec 1156-18 Dec 1157		21	19 Dec 1174-18 Dec 1175
4	19 Dec 1157-18 Dec 1158		22	19 Dec 1175-18 Dec 1176
5	19 Dec 1158-18 Dec 1159		23	19 Dec 1176-18 Dec 1177
6	19 Dec 1159-18 Dec 1160		24	19 Dec 1177-18 Dec 1178
7	19 Dec 1160-18 Dec 1161		25	19 Dec 1178-18 Dec 1179
8	19 Dec 1161-18 Dec 1162		26	19 Dec 1179-18 Dec 1180
9	19 Dec 1162-18 Dec 1163		27	19 Dec 1180-18 Dec 1181
10	19 Dec 1163-18 Dec 1164		28	19 Dec 1181-18 Dec 1182
11	19 Dec 1164-18 Dec 1165		29	19 Dec 1182-18 Dec 1183
12	19 Dec 1165-18 Dec 1166		30	19 Dec 1183-18 Dec 1184
13	19 Dec 1166-18 Dec 1167		31	19 Dec 1184-18 Dec 1185
14	19 Dec 1167-18 Dec 1168		32	19 Dec 1185-18 Dec 1186
15	19 Dec 1168-18 Dec 1169		33	19 Dec 1186-18 Dec 1187
16	19 Dec 1169-18 Dec 1170		34	19 Dec 1187-18 Dec 1188
17	19 Dec 1170-18 Dec 1171		35	19 Dec 1188- 6 Jul 1189
18	19 Dec 1171-18 Dec 1172			

RICHARD I

1	3 Sep 1189- 2 Sep 1190		6	3 Sep 1194- 2 Sep 1195
2	3 Sep 1190- 2 Sep 1191		7	3 Sep 1195- 2 Sep 1196
3	3 Sep 1191- 2 Sep 1192		8	3 Sep 1196- 2 Sep 1197
4	3 Sep 1192- 2 Sep 1193		9	3 Sep 1197- 2 Sep 1198
5	3 Sep 1193- 2 Sep 1194		10	3 Sep 1198- 6 Apr 1199

JOHN

1	27 May 1190-17 May 1200		10	15 May 1208- 6 May 1209
2	18 May 1200- 2 May 1201		11	7 May 1209-26 May 1210
3	3 May 1201-22 May 1202		12	27 May 1210-11 May 1211
4	23 May 1202-14 May 1203		13	12 May 1211- 2 May 1212
5	15 May 1203- 2 Jun 1204		14	3 May 1212-22 May 1213
6	3 Jun 1204-18 May 1205		15	23 May 1213- 7 May 1214
7	19 May 1205-10 May 1206		16	8 May 1214-27 May 1215
8	11 May 1206-30 May 1207		17	28 May 1215-18 May 1216
9	31 May 1207-14 May 1208		18	19 May 1216-19 Oct 1216

HENRY III

1	28 Oct 1216-27 Oct 1217	30	28 Oct 1245-27 Oct 1246
2	28 Oct 1217-27 Oct 1218	31	28 Oct 1246-27 Oct 1247
3	28 Oct 1218-27 Oct 1219	32	28 Oct 1247-27 Oct 1248
4	28 Oct 1219-27 Oct 1220	33	28 Oct 1248-27 Oct 1249
5	28 Oct 1220-27 Oct 1221	34	28 Oct 1249-27 Oct 1250
6	28 Oct 1221-27 Oct 1222	35	28 Oct 1250-27 Oct 1251
7	28 Oct 1222-27 Oct 1223	36	28 Oct 1251-27 Oct 1252
8	28 Oct 1223-27 Oct 1224	37	28 Oct 1252-27 Oct 1253
9	28 Oct 1224-27 Oct 1225	38	28 Oct 1253-27 Oct 1254
10	28 Oct 1225-27 Oct 1226	39	28 Oct 1254-27 Oct 1255
11	28 Oct 1226-27 Oct 1227	40	28 Oct 1255-27 Oct 1256
12	28 Oct 1227-27 Oct 1228	41	28 Oct 1256-27 Oct 1257
13	28 Oct 1228-27 Oct 1229	42	28 Oct 1257-27 Oct 1258
14	28 Oct 1229-27 Oct 1230	43	28 Oct 1258-27 Oct 1259
15	28 Oct 1230-27 Oct 1231	44	28 Oct 1259-27 Oct 1260
16	28 Oct 1231-27 Oct 1232	45	28 Oct 1260-27 Oct 1261
17	28 Oct 1232-27 Oct 1233	46	28 Oct 1261-27 Oct 1262
18	28 Oct 1233-27 Oct 1234	47	28 Oct 1262-27 Oct 1263
19	28 Oct 1234-27 Oct 1235	48	28 Oct 1263-27 Oct 1264
20	28 Oct 1235-27 Oct 1236	49	28 Oct 1264-27 Oct 1265
21	28 Oct 1236-27 Oct 1237	50	28 Oct 1265-27 Oct 1266
22	28 Oct 1237-27 Oct 1238	51	28 Oct 1266-27 Oct 1267
23	28 Oct 1238-27 Oct 1239	52	28 Oct 1267-27 Oct 1268
24	28 Oct 1239-27 Oct 1240	53	28 Oct 1268-27 Oct 1269
25	28 Oct 1240-27 Oct 1241	54	28 Oct 1269-27 Oct 1270
26	28 Oct 1241-27 Oct 1242	55	28 Oct 1270-27 Oct 1271
27	28 Oct 1242-27 Oct 1243	56	28 Oct 1271-27 Oct 1272
28	28 Oct 1243-27 Oct 1244	57	28 Oct 1272-16 Nov1272
29	28 Oct 1244-27 Oct 1245		

EDWARD I

1	20 Nov 1272-19 Nov 1273		19	20 Nov 1290-19 Nov 1291
2	20 Nov 1273-19 Nov 1274		20	20 Nov 1291-19 Nov 1292
3	20 Nov 1274-19 Nov 1275		21	20 Nov 1292-19 Nov 1293
4	20 Nov 1275-19 Nov 1276		22	20 Nov 1293-19 Nov 1294
5	20 Nov 1276-19 Nov 1277		23	20 Nov 1294-19 Nov 1295
6	20 Nov 1277-19 Nov 1278		24	20 Nov 1295-19 Nov 1296
7	20 Nov 1278-19 Nov 1279		25	20 Nov 1296-19 Nov 1297
8	20 Nov 1279-19 Nov 1280		26	20 Nov 1297-19 Nov 1298
9	20 Nov 1280-19 Nov 1281		27	20 Nov 1298-19 Nov1299
10	20 Nov 1281-19 Nov 1282		28	20 Nov 1299-19 Nov 1300
11	20 Nov 1282-19 Nov 1283		29	20 Nov 1300-19 Nov 1301
12	20 Nov 1283-19 Nov 1284		30	20 Nov 1301-19 Nov 1302
13	20 Nov 1284-19 Nov 1285		31	20 Nov 1302-19 Nov 1303
14	20 Nov 1285-19 Nov 1286		32	20 Nov 1303-19 Nov 1304
15	20 Nov 1286-19 Nov 1287		33	20 Nov 1304-19 Nov 1305
16	20 Nov 1287-19 Nov 1288		34	20 Nov 1305-19 Nov 1306
17	20 Nov 1288-19 Nov 1289		35	20 Nov 1306- 7 Jul 1307
18	20 Nov 1289-19 Nov1290			

EDWARD II

1	8 Jul 1307-7 Jul 1308		11	8 Jul 1317- 7 Jul 1318
2	8 Jul 1308-7 Jul 1309		12	8 Jul 1318- 7 Jul 1319
3	8 Jul 1309-7 Jul 1310		13	8 Jul 1319- 7 Jul 1320
4	8 Jul 1310-7 Jul 1311		14	8 Jul 1320- 7 Jul 1321
5	8 Jul 1311-7 Jul 1312		15	8 Jul 1321- 7 Jul 1322
6	8 Jul 1312-7 Jul 1313		16	8 Jul 1322- 7 Jul 1323
7	8 Jul 1313-7 Jul 1314		17	8 Jul 1323- 7 Jul 1324
8	8 Jul 1314-7 Jul 1315		18	8 Jul 1324- 7 Jul 1325
9	8 Jul 1315-7 Jul 1316		19	8 Jul 1325- 7 Jul 1326
10	8 Jul 1316-7 Jul 1317		20	8 Jul 1326-20 Jan 1327

EDWARD III

1	25 Jan 1327-24 Jan 1328	27	25 Jan 1353-24 Jan 1354
2	25 Jan 1328-24 Jan 1329	28	25 Jan 1354-24 Jan 1355
3	25 Jan 1329-24 Jan 1330	29	25 Jan 1355-24 Jan 1356
4	25 Jan 1330-24 Jan 1331	30	25 Jan 1356-24 Jan 1357
5	25 Jan 1331-24 Jan 1332	31	25 Jan 1357-24 Jan 1358
6	25 Jan 1332-24 Jan 1333	32	25 Jan 1358-24 Jan 1359
7	25 Jan 1333-24 Jan 1334	33	25 Jan 1359-24 Jan 1360
8	25 Jan 1334-24 Jan 1335	34	25 Jan 1360-24 Jan 1361
9	25 Jan 1335-24 Jan 1336	35	25 Jan 1361-24 Jan 1362
10	25 Jan 1336-24 Jan 1337	36	25 Jan 1362-24 Jan 1363
11	25 Jan 1337-24 Jan 1338	37	25 Jan 1363-24 Jan 1364
12	25 Jan 1338-24 Jan 1339	38	25 Jan 1364-24 Jan 1365
13	25 Jan 1339-24 Jan 1340	39	25 Jan 1365-24 Jan 1366
14	25 Jan 1340-24 Jan 1341	40	25 Jan 1366-24 Jan 1367
15	25 Jan 1341-24 Jan 1342	41	25 Jan 1367-24 Jan 1368
16	25 Jan 1342-24 Jan 1343	42	25 Jan 1368-24 Jan 1369
17	25 Jan 1343-24 Jan 1344	43	25 Jan 1369-24 Jan 1370
18	25 Jan 1344-24 Jan 1345	44	25 Jan 1370-24 Jan 1371
19	25 Jan 1345-24 Jan 1346	45	25 Jan 1371-24 Jan 1372
20	25 Jan 1346-24 Jan 1347	46	25 Jan 1372-24 Jan 1373
21	25 Jan 1347-24 Jan 1348	47	25 Jan 1373-24 Jan 1374
22	25 Jan 1348-24 Jan 1349	48	25 Jan 1374-24 Jan 1375
23	25 Jan 1349-24 Jan 1350	49	25 Jan 1375-24 Jan 1376
24	25 Jan 1350-24 Jan 1351	50	25 Jan 1376-24 Jan 1377
25	25 Jan 1351-24 Jan 1352	51	25 Jan 1377-21 Jun 1377
26	25 Jan 1352-24 Jan 1353		

RICHARD II

1	22 Jun 1377-21 Jun 1378	13	22 Jun 1389-21 Jun 1390
2	22 Jun 1378-21 Jun 1379	14	22 Jun 1390-21 Jun 1391
3	22 Jun 1379-21 Jun 1380	15	22 Jun 1391-21 Jun 1392
4	22 Jun 1380-21 Jun 1381	16	22 Jun 1392-21 Jun 1393
5	22 Jun 1381-21 Jun 1382	17	22 Jun 1393-21 Jun 1394
6	22 Jun 1382-21 Jun 1383	18	22 Jun 1394-21 Jun 1395
7	22 Jun 1383-21 Jun 1384	19	22 Jun 1395-21 Jun 1396
8	22 Jun 1384-21 Jun 1385	20	22 Jun 1396-21 Jun 1397
9	22 Jun 1385-21 Jun 1386	21	22 Jun 1397-21 Jun 1398
10	22 Jun 1386-21 Jun 1387	22	22 Jun 1398-21 Jun 1399
11	22 Jun 1387-21 Jun 1388	23	22 Jun 1399-29 Sep 1399
12	22 Jun 1388-21 Jun 1389		

HENRY IV

1	30 Sep 1399-29 Sep 1400		8	30 Sep 1406-29 Sep 1407
2	30 Sep 1400-29 Sep 1401		9	30 Sep 1407-29 Sep 1408
3	30 Sep 1401-29 Sep 1402		10	30 Sep 1408-29 Sep 1409
4	30 Sep 1402-29 Sep 1403		11	30 Sep 1409-29 Sep 1410
5	30 Sep 1403-29 Sep 1404		12	30 Sep 1410-29 Sep 1411
6	30 Sep 1404-29 Sep 1405		13	30 Sep 1411-29 Sep 1412
7	30 Sep 1405-29 Sep 1406		14	30 Sep 1412-20 Mar 1413

HENRY V

1	21 Mar 1413-20 Mar 1414		6	21 Mar 1418-20 Mar 1419
2	21 Mar 1414-20 Mar 1415		7	21 Mar 1419-20 Mar 1420
3	21 Mar 1415-20 Mar 1416		8	21 Mar 1420-20 Mar 1421
4	21 Mar 1416-20 Mar 1417		9	21 Mar 1421-20 Mar 1422
5	21 Mar 1417-20 Mar 1418		10	21 Mar 1422-31 Aug 1422

HENRY VI

1	1 Sep 1422-31 Aug 1423		22	1 Sep 1443-31 Aug 1444
2	1 Sep 1423-31 Aug 1424		23	1 Sep 1444-31 Aug 1445
3	1 Sep 1424-31 Aug 1425		24	1 Sep 1445-31 Aug 1446
4	1 Sep 1425-31 Aug 1426		25	1 Sep 1446-31 Aug 1447
5	1 Sep 1426-31 Aug 1427		26	1 Sep 1447-31 Aug 1448
6	1 Sep 1427-31 Aug 1428		27	1 Sep 1448-31 Aug 1449
7	1 Sep 1428-31 Aug 1429		28	1 Sep 1449-31 Aug 1450
8	1 Sep 1429-31 Aug 1430		29	1 Sep 1450-31 Aug 1451
9	1 Sep 1430-31 Aug 1431		30	1 Sep 1451-31 Aug 1452
10	1 Sep 1431-31 Aug 1432		31	1 Sep 1452-31 Aug 1453
11	1 Sep 1432-31 Aug 1433		32	1 Sep 1453-31 Aug 1454
12	1 Sep 1433-31 Aug 1434		33	1 Sep 1454-31 Aug 1455
13	1 Sep 1434-31 Aug 1435		34	1 Sep 1455-31 Aug 1456
14	1 Sep 1435-31 Aug 1436		35	1 Sep 1456-31 Aug 1457
15	1 Sep 1436-31 Aug 1437		36	1 Sep 1457-31 Aug 1458
16	1 Sep 1437-31 Aug 1438		37	1 Sep 1458-31 Aug 1459
17	1 Sep 1438-31 Aug 1439		38	1 Sep 1459-31 Aug 1460
18	1 Sep 1439-31 Aug 1440		39	1 Sep 1460-4 Mar 1461
19	1 Sep 1440-31 Aug 1441			*and*
20	1 Sep 1441-31 Aug 1442		49	9 Oct 1470-11 Apr 1471
21	1 Sep 1442-31 Aug 1443			

EDWARD IV

1	4 Mar 1461-3 Mar 1462		13	4 Mar 1473-3 Mar 1474
2	4 Mar 1462-3 Mar 1463		14	4 Mar 1474-3 Mar 1475
3	4 Mar 1463-3 Mar 1464		15	4 Mar 1475-3 Mar 1476
4	4 Mar 1464-3 Mar 1465		16	4 Mar 1476-3 Mar 1477
5	4 Mar 1465-3 Mar 1466		17	4 Mar 1477-3 Mar 1478
6	4 Mar 1466-3 Mar 1467		18	4 Mar 1478-3 Mar 1479
7	4 Mar 1467-3 Mar 1468		19	4 Mar 1479-3 Mar 1480
8	4 Mar 1468-3 Mar 1469		20	4 Mar 1480-3 Mar 1481
9	4 Mar 1469-3 Mar 1470		21	4 Mar 1481-3 Mar 1482
10	4 Mar 1470-3 Mar 1471		22	4 Mar 1482-3 Mar 1483
11	4 Mar 1471-3 Mar 1472		23	4 Mar 1483-9 Apr 1483
12	4 Mar 1472-3 Mar 1473			

N.B. These regnal years are nominal in the case of nos. 10 and 11, because of the political circumstances explained on p.48

EDWARD V

1	9 Apr 1483-25 Jun 1483

RICHARD III

1	26 Jun 1483-25 Jun 1484		3	26 Jun 1485-22 Aug 1485
2	26 Jun 1484-25 Jun 1485			

HENRY VII

1	22 Aug 1485-21 Aug 1486		13	22 Aug 1497-21 Aug 1498
2	22 Aug 1486-21 Aug 1487		14	22 Aug 1498-21 Aug 1499
3	22 Aug 1487-21 Aug 1488		15	22 Aug 1499-21 Aug 1500
4	22 Aug 1488-21 Aug 1489		16	22 Aug 1500-21 Aug 1501
5	22 Aug 1489-21 Aug 1490		17	22 Aug 1501-21 Aug 1502
6	22 Aug 1490-21 Aug 1491		18	22 Aug 1502-21 Aug 1503
7	22 Aug 1491-21 Aug 1492		19	22 Aug 1503-21 Aug 1504
8	22 Aug 1492-21 Aug 1493		20	22 Aug 1504-21 Aug 1505
9	22 Aug 1493-21 Aug 1494		21	22 Aug 1505-21 Aug 1506
10	22 Aug 1494-21 Aug 1495		22	22 Aug 1506-21 Aug 1507
11	22 Aug 1495-21 Aug 1496		23	22 Aug 1507-21 Aug 1508
12	22 Aug 1496-21 Aug 1497		24	22 Aug 1508-21 Apr 1509

HENRY VIII

1	22 Apr 1509-21 Apr 1510		20	22 Apr 1528-21 Apr 1529
2	22 Apr 1510-21 Apr 1511		21	22 Apr 1529-21 Apr 1530
3	22 Apr 1511-21 Apr 1512		22	22 Apr 1530-21 Apr 1531
4	22 Apr 1512-21 Apr 1513		23	22 Apr 1531-21 Apr 1532
5	22 Apr 1513-21 Apr 1514		24	22 Apr 1532-21 Apr 1533
6	22 Apr 1514-21 Apr 1515		25	22 Apr 1533-21 Apr 1534
7	22 Apr 1515-21 Apr 1516		26	22 Apr 1534-21 Apr 1535
8	22 Apr 1516-21 Apr 1517		27	22 Apr 1535-21 Apr 1536
9	22 Apr 1517-21 Apr 1518		28	22 Apr 1536-21 Apr 1537
10	22 Apr 1518-21 Apr 1519		29	22 Apr 1537-21 Apr 1538
11	22 Apr 1519-21 Apr 1520		30	22 Apr 1538-21 Apr 1539
12	22 Apr 1520-21 Apr 1521		31	22 Apr 1539-21 Apr 1540
13	22 Apr 1521-21 Apr 1522		32	22 Apr 1540-21 Apr 1541
14	22 Apr 1522-21 Apr 1523		33	22 Apr 1541-21 Apr 1542
15	22 Apr 1523-21 Apr 1524		34	22 Apr 1542-21 Apr 1543
16	22 Apr 1524-21 Apr 1525		35	22 Apr 1543-21 Apr 1544
17	22 Apr 1525-21 Apr 1526		36	22 Apr 1544-21 Apr 1545
18	22 Apr 1526-21 Apr 1527		37	22 Apr 1545-21 Apr 1546
19	22 Apr 1527-21 Apr 1528		38	22 Apr 1546-28 Jan 1547

EDWARD VI

1	28 Jan 1547-27 Jan 1548		5	28 Jan 1551-27 Jan 1552
2	28 Jan 1548-27 Jan 1549		6	28 Jan 1552-27 Jan 1553
3	28 Jan 1549-27 Jan 1550		7	28 Jan 1553- 6 Jul 1553
4	28 Jan 1550-27 Jan 1551			

JANE

1	6 Jul 1553-19 Jul 1553

MARY I

1	19 Jul 1553-5 July 1554		2	6 Jul 1554-24 Jul 1554

PHILIP AND MARY

1 & 2	25 Jul 1554- 5 Jul 1555		3 & 5	6 Jul 1557-24 Jul 1557
1 & 3	6 Jul 1555-24 Jul 1555		4 & 5	25 Jul 1557- 5 Jul 1558
2 & 3	25 Jul 1555- 5 Jul 1556		4 & 6	6 Jul 1558-24 Jul 1558
2 & 4	6 Jul 1556-24 Jul 1556		5 & 6	25 Jul 1558-17 Nov1558
3 & 4	25 Jul 1556- 5 Jul 1557			

ELIZABETH I

1	17 Nov 1558-16 Nov 1559	24	17 Nov 1581-16 Nov 1582
2	17 Nov 1559-16 Nov 1560	25	17 Nov 1582-16 Nov 1583
3	17 Nov 1560-16 Nov 1561	26	17 Nov 1583-16 Nov 1584
4	17 Nov 1561-16 Nov 1562	27	17 Nov 1584-16 Nov 1585
5	17 Nov 1562-16 Nov 1563	28	17 Nov 1585-16 Nov 1586
6	17 Nov 1563-16 Nov 1564	29	17 Nov 1586-16 Nov 1587
7	17 Nov 1564-16 Nov 1565	30	17 Nov 1587-16 Nov 1588
8	17 Nov 1565-16 Nov 1566	31	17 Nov 1588-16 Nov 1589
9	17 Nov 1566-16 Nov 1567	32	17 Nov 1589-16 Nov 1590
10	17 Nov 1567-16 Nov 1568	33	17 Nov 1590-16 Nov 1591
11	17 Nov 1568-16 Nov 1569	34	17 Nov 1591-16 Nov 1592
12	17 Nov 1569-16 Nov 1570	35	17 Nov 1592-16 Nov 1593
13	17 Nov 1570-16 Nov 1571	36	17 Nov 1593-16 Nov 1594
14	17 Nov 1571-16 Nov 1572	37	17 Nov 1594-16 Nov 1595
15	17 Nov 1572-16 Nov 1573	38	17 Nov 1595-16 Nov 1596
16	17 Nov 1573-16 Nov 1574	39	17 Nov 1596-16 Nov 1597
17	17 Nov 1574-16 Nov 1575	40	17 Nov 1597-16 Nov 1598
18	17 Nov 1575-16 Nov 1576	41	17 Nov 1598-16 Nov 1599
19	17 Nov 1576-16 Nov 1577	42	17 Nov 1599-16 Nov 1600
20	17 Nov 1577-16 Nov 1578	43	17 Nov 1600-16 Nov 1601
21	17 Nov 1578-16 Nov 1579	44	17 Nov 1601-16 Nov 1602
22	17 Nov 1579-16 Nov 1580	45	17 Nov 1602-24 Mar 1603
23	17 Nov 1580-16 Nov 1581		

JAMES I

1	24 Mar 1603-23 Mar 1604	13	24 Mar 1615-23 Mar 1616
2	24 Mar 1604-23 Mar 1605	14	24 Mar 1616-23 Mar 1617
3	24 Mar 1605-23 Mar 1606	15	24 Mar 1617-23 Mar 1618
4	24 Mar 1606-23 Mar 1607	16	24 Mar 1618-23 Mar 1619
5	24 Mar 1607-23 Mar 1608	17	24 Mar 1619-23 Mar 1620
6	24 Mar 1608-23 Mar 1609	18	24 Mar 1620-23 Mar 1621
7	24 Mar 1609-23 Mar 1610	19	24 Mar 1621-23 Mar 1622
8	24 Mar 1610-23 Mar 1611	20	24 Mar 1622-23 Mar 1623
9	24 Mar 1611-23 Mar 1612	21	24 Mar 1623-23 Mar 1624
10	24 Mar 1612-23 Mar 1613	22	24 Mar 1624-23 Mar 1625
11	24 Mar 1613-23 Mar 1614	23	24 Mar 1625-27 Mar 1625
12	24 Mar 1614-23 Mar 1615		

CHARLES I

1	27 Mar 1625-26 Mar 1626	13	27 Mar 1637-26 Mar 1638
2	27 Mar 1626-26 Mar 1627	14	27 Mar 1638-26 Mar 1639
3	27 Mar 1627-26 Mar 1628	15	27 Mar 1639-26 Mar 1640
4	27 Mar 1628-26 Mar 1629	16	27 Mar 1640-26 Mar 1641
5	27 Mar 1629-26 Mar 1630	17	27 Mar 1641-26 Mar 1642
6	27 Mar 1630-26 Mar 1631	18	27 Mar 1642-26 Mar 1643
7	27 Mar 1631-26 Mar 1632	19	27 Mar 1643-26 Mar 1644
8	27 Mar 1632-26 Mar 1633	20	27 Mar 1644-26 Mar 1645
9	27 Mar 1633-26 Mar 1634	21	27 Mar 1645-26 Mar 1646
10	27 Mar 1634-26 Mar 1635	22	27 Mar 1646-26 Mar 1647
11	27 Mar 1635-26 Mar 1636	23	27 Mar 1647-26 Mar 1648
12	27 Mar 1636-26 Mar 1637	24	27 Mar 1648-30 Jan 1649

CHARLES II

12	29 May 1660-29 Jan 1661	27	30 Jan 1675-29 Jan 1676
13	30 Jan 1661-29 Jan 1662	28	30 Jan 1676-29 Jan 1677
14	30 Jan 1662-29 Jan 1663	29	30 Jan 1677-29 Jan 1678
15	30 Jan 1663-29 Jan 1664	30	30 Jan 1678-29 Jan 1679
16	30 Jan 1664-29 Jan 1665	31	30 Jan 1679-29 Jan 1680
17	30 Jan 1665-29 Jan 1666	32	30 Jan 1680-29 Jan 1681
18	30 Jan 1666-29 Jan 1667	33	30 Jan 1681-29 Jan 1682
19	30 Jan 1667-29 Jan 1668	34	30 Jan 1682-29 Jan 1683
20	30 Jan 1668-29 Jan 1669	35	30 Jan 1683-29 Jan 1684
21	30 Jan 1669-29 Jan 1670	36	30 Jan 1684-29 Jan 1685
22	30 Jan 1670-29 Jan 1671	37	30 Jan 1685- 6 Feb 1685
23	30 Jan 1671-29 Jan 1672		
24	30 Jan 1672-29 Jan 1673		
25	30 Jan 1673-29 Jan 1674		
26	30 Jan 1674-29 Jan 1675		

JAMES II

1	6 Feb 1685-5 Feb 1686	3	6 Feb 1687- 5 Feb 1688
2	6 Feb 1686-5 Feb 1687	4	6 Feb 1688-11 Dec 1688

Interregnum   12 Dec 1688-12 Feb 1689

WILLIAM AND MARY

1	13 Feb 1689-12 Feb 1690	4	13 Feb 1692-12 Feb 1693
2	13 Feb 1690-12 Feb 1691	5	13 Feb 1693-12 Feb 1694
3	13 Feb 1691-12 Feb 1692	6	13 Feb 1694-27 Dec 1694

WILLIAM III

6	28 Dec 1694-12 Feb 1695	11	13 Feb 1699-12 Feb 1700
7	13 Feb 1695-12 Feb 1696	12	13 Feb 1700-12 Feb 1701
8	13 Feb 1696-12 Feb 1697	13	13 Feb 1701-12 Feb 1702
9	13 Feb 1697-12 Feb 1698	14	13 Feb 1702- 8 Mar 1702
10	13 Feb 1698-12 Feb 1699		

ANNE

1	8 Mar 1702-7 Mar 1703	8	8 Mar 1709-7 Mar 1710
2	8 Mar 1703-7 Mar 1704	9	8 Mar 1710-7 Mar 1711
3	8 Mar 1704-7 Mar 1705	10	8 Mar 1711-7 Mar 1712
4	8 Mar 1705-7 Mar 1706	11	8 Mar 1712-7 Mar 1713
5	8 Mar 1706-7 Mar 1707	12	8 Mar 1713-7 Mar 1714
6	8 Mar 1707-7 Mar 1708	13	8 Mar 1714-1 Aug 1714
7	8 Mar 1708-7 Mar 1709		

GEORGE I

1	1 Aug 1714-31 Jul 1715	8	1 Aug 1721-31 Jul 1722
2	1 Aug 1715-31 Jul 1716	9	1 Aug 1722-31 Jul 1723
3	1 Aug 1716-31 Jul 1717	10	1 Aug 1723-31 Jul 1724
4	1 Aug 1717-31 Jul 1718	11	1 Aug 1724-31 Jul 1725
5	1 Aug 1718-31 Jul 1719	12	1 Aug 1725-31 Jul 1726
6	1 Aug 1719-31 Jul 1720	13	1 Aug 1726-11 Jun 1727
7	1 Aug 1720-31 Jul 1721		

23. In 1714 the British government offered a reward of £20,000 for a timekeeper that would not be more than two minutes out at the end of a voyage to the West Indies. John Harrison (1693-1776) was determined the win the money and this is the second of his revolutionary and innovative prototypes, produced in 1739.

GEORGE II

1	11 Jun 1727-10 Jun 1728	18	11 Jun 1744-10 Jun 1745
2	11 Jun 1728-10 Jun 1729	19	11 Jun 1745-10 Jun 1746
3	11 Jun 1729-10 Jun 1730	20	11 Jun 1746-10 Jun 1747
4	11 Jun 1730-10 Jun 1731	21	11 Jun 1747-10 Jun 1748
5	11 Jun 1731-10 Jun 1732	22	11 Jun 1748-10 Jun 1749
6	11 Jun 1732-10 Jun 1733	23	11 Jun 1749-10 Jun 1750
7	11 Jun 1733-10 Jun 1734	24	11 Jun 1750-10 Jun 1751
8	11 Jun 1734-10 Jun 1735	25	11 Jun 1751-10 Jun 1752
9	11 Jun 1735-10 Jun 1736	26	11 Jun 1752-21 Jun 1753
10	11 Jun 1736-10 Jun 1737	27	22 Jun 1753-21 Jun 1754
11	11 Jun 1737-10 Jun 1738	28	22 Jun 1754-21 Jun 1755
12	11 Jun 1738-10 Jun 1739	29	22 Jun 1755-21 Jun 1756
13	11 Jun 1739-10 Jun 1740	30	22 Jun 1756-21 Jun 1757
14	11 Jun 1740-10 Jun 1741	31	22 Jun 1757-21 Jun 1758
15	11 Jun 1741-10 Jun 1742	32	22 Jun 1758-21 Jun 1759
16	11 Jun 1742-10 Jun 1743	33	22 Jun 1759-21 Jun 1760
17	11 Jun 1743-10 Jun 1744	34	22 Jun 1760-25 Oct 1760

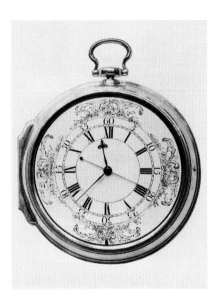

24. This is Harrison's fourth timekeeper, dramatically reduced in scale from the prototype version shown in the previous illustration - it was small enough to be held in the hand. It erred by only five seconds (corresponding to an error of 1.5 miles in longitude) after a voyage to the West Indies in 1761-2. However, although he had amply fulfilled the conditions of the 1714 offer, Harrison was not paid the award in full until 1773.

GEORGE III

1	25 Oct 1760-24 Oct 1761	31	25 Oct 1790-24 Oct 1791
2	25 Oct 1761-24 Oct 1762	32	25 Oct 1791-24 Oct 1792
3	25 Oct 1762-24 Oct 1763	33	25 Oct 1792-24 Oct 1793
4	25 Oct 1763-24 Oct 1764	34	25 Oct 1793-24 Oct 1794
5	25 Oct 1764-24 Oct 1765	35	25 Oct 1794-24 Oct 1795
6	25 Oct 1765-24 Oct 1766	36	25 Oct 1795-24 Oct 1796
7	25 Oct 1766-24 Oct 1767	37	25 Oct 1796-24 Oct 1797
8	25 Oct 1767-24 Oct 1768	38	25 Oct 1797-24 Oct 1798
9	25 Oct 1768-24 Oct 1769	39	25 Oct 1798-24 Oct 1799
10	25 Oct 1769-24 Oct 1770	40	25 Oct 1799-24 Oct 1800
11	25 Oct 1770-24 Oct 1771	41	25 Oct 1800-24 Oct 1801
12	25 Oct 1771-24 Oct 1772	42	25 Oct 1801-24 Oct 1802
13	25 Oct 1772-24 Oct 1773	43	25 Oct 1802-24 Oct 1803
14	25 Oct 1773-24 Oct 1774	44	25 Oct 1803-24 Oct 1804
15	25 Oct 1774-24 Oct 1775	45	25 Oct 1804-24 Oct 1805
16	25 Oct 1775-24 Oct 1776	46	25 Oct 1805-24 Oct 1806
17	25 Oct 1776-24 Oct 1777	47	25 Oct 1806-24 Oct 1807
18	25 Oct 1777-24 Oct 1778	48	25 Oct 1807-24 Oct 1808
19	25 Oct 1778-24 Oct 1779	49	25 Oct 1808-24 Oct 1809
20	25 Oct 1779-24 Oct 1780	50	25 Oct 1809-24 Oct 1810
21	25 Oct 1780-24 Oct 1781	51	25 Oct 1810-24 Oct 1811
22	25 Oct 1781-24 Oct 1782	52	25 Oct 1811-24 Oct 1812
23	25 Oct 1782-24 Oct 1783	53	25 Oct 1812-24 Oct 1813
24	25 Oct 1783-24 Oct 1784	54	25 Oct 1813-24 Oct 1814
25	25 Oct 1784-24 Oct 1785	55	25 Oct 1814-24 Oct 1815
26	25 Oct 1785-24 Oct 1786	56	25 Oct 1815-24 Oct 1816
27	25 Oct 1786-24 Oct 1787	57	25 Oct 1816-24 Oct 1817
28	25 Oct 1787-24 Oct 1788	58	25 Oct 1817-24 Oct 1818
29	25 Oct 1788-24 Oct 1789	59	25 Oct 1818-24 Oct 1819
30	25 Oct 1789-24 Oct 1790	60	25 Oct 1819-29 Jan 1820

GEORGE IV

1	29 Jan 1820-28 Jan 1821	7	29 Jan 1826-28 Jan 1827
2	29 Jan 1821-28 Jan 1822	8	29 Jan 1827-28 Jan 1828
3	29 Jan 1822-28 Jan 1823	9	29 Jan 1828-28 Jan 1829
4	29 Jan 1823-28 Jan 1824	10	29 Jan 1829-28 Jan 1830
5	29 Jan 1824-28 Jan 1825	11	29 Jan 1830-26 Jun 1830
6	29 Jan 1825-28 Jan 1826		

WILLIAM IV

1	26 Jun 1830-25 Jun 1831		5	26 Jun 1834-25 Jun 1835
2	26 Jun 1831-25 Jun 1832		6	26 Jun 1835-25 Jun 1836
3	26 Jun 1832-25 Jun 1833		7	26 Jun 1836-20 Jun 1837
4	26 Jun 1833-25 Jun 1834			

VICTORIA

1	20 Jun 1837-19 Jun 1838		33	20 Jun 1869-19 Jun 1870
2	20 Jun 1838-19 Jun 1839		34	20 Jun 1870-19 Jun 1871
3	20 Jun 1839-19 Jun 1840		35	20 Jun 1871-19 Jun 1872
4	20 Jun 1840-19 Jun 1841		36	20 Jun 1872-19 Jun 1873
5	20 Jun 1841-19 Jun 1842		37	20 Jun 1873-19 Jun 1874
6	20 Jun 1842-19 Jun 1843		38	20 Jun 1874-19 Jun 1875
7	20 Jun 1843-19 Jun 1844		39	20 Jun 1875-19 Jun 1876
8	20 Jun 1844-19 Jun 1845		40	20 Jun 1876-19 Jun 1877
9	20 Jun 1845-19 Jun 1846		41	20 Jun 1877-19 Jun 1878
10	20 Jun 1846-19 Jun 1847		42	20 Jun 1878-19 Jun 1879
11	20 Jun 1847-19 Jun 1848		43	20 Jun 1879-19 Jun 1880
12	20 Jun 1848-19 Jun 1849		44	20 Jun 1880-19 Jun 1881
13	20 Jun 1849-19 Jun 1850		45	20 Jun 1881-19 Jun 1882
14	20 Jun 1850-19 Jun 1851		46	20 Jun 1882-19 Jun 1883
15	20 Jun 1851-19 Jun 1852		47	20 Jun 1883-19 Jun 1884
16	20 Jun 1852-19 Jun 1853		48	20 Jun 1884-19 Jun 1885
17	20 Jun 1853-19 Jun 1854		49	20 Jun 1885-19 Jun 1886
18	20 Jun 1854-19 Jun 1855		50	20 Jun 1886-19 Jun 1887
19	20 Jun 1855-19 Jun 1856		51	20 Jun 1887-19 Jun 1888
20	20 Jun 1856-19 Jun 1857		52	20 Jun 1888-19 Jun 1889
21	20 Jun 1857-19 Jun 1858		53	20 Jun 1889-19 Jun 1890
22	20 Jun 1858-19 Jun 1859		54	20 Jun 1890-19 Jun 1891
23	20 Jun 1859-19 Jun 1860		55	20 Jun 1891-19 Jun 1892
24	20 Jun 1860-19 Jun 1861		56	20 Jun 1892-19 Jun 1893
25	20 Jun 1861-19 Jun 1862		57	20 Jun 1893-19 Jun 1894
26	20 Jun 1862-19 Jun 1863		58	20 Jun 1894-19 Jun 1895
27	20 Jun 1863-19 Jun 1864		59	20 Jun 1895-19 Jun 1896
28	20 Jun 1864-19 Jun 1865		60	20 Jun 1896-19 Jun 1897
29	20 Jun 1865-19 Jun 1866		61	20 Jun 1897-19 Jun 1898
30	20 Jun 1866-19 Jun 1867		62	20 Jun 1898-19 Jun 1899
31	20 Jun 1867-19 Jun 1868		63	20 Jun 1899-19 Jun 1900
32	20 Jun 1868-19 Jun 1869		64	20 Jun 1900-22 Jan 1901

EDWARD VII

1	22 Jan 1901-21 Jan 1902		6	22 Jan 1906-21 Jan 1907
2	22 Jan 1902-21 Jan 1903		7	22 Jan 1907-21 Jan 1908
3	22 Jan 1903-21 Jan 1904		8	22 Jan 1908-21 Jan 1909
4	22 Jan 1904-21 Jan 1905		9	22 Jan 1909-21 Jan 1910
5	22 Jan 1905-21 Jan 1906		10	22 Jan 1910- 6 May 1910

GEORGE V

1	6 May 1910- 5 May 1911		14	6 May 1923- 5 May 1924
2	6 May 1911- 5 May 1912		15	6 May 1924- 5 May 1925
3	6 May 1912- 5 May 1913		16	6 May 1925- 5 May 1926
4	6 May 1913- 5 May 1914		17	6 May 1926- 5 May 1927
5	6 May 1914- 5 May 1915		18	6 May 1927- 5 May 1928
6	6 May 1915- 5 May 1916		19	6 May 1928- 5 May 1929
7	6 May 1916- 5 May 1917		20	6 May 1929- 5 May 1930
8	6 May 1917- 5 May 1918		21	6 May 1930- 5 May 1931
9	6 May 1918- 5 May 1919		22	6 May 1931- 5 May 1932
10	6 May 1919- 5 May 1920		23	6 May 1932- 5 May 1933
11	6 May 1920- 5 May 1921		24	6 May 1933- 5 May 1934
12	6 May 1921- 5 May 1922		25	6 May 1934- 5 May 1935
13	6 May 1922- 5 May 1923		26	6 May 1935-20 Jan 1936

EDWARD VIII

1	20 Jan 1936-11 Dec 1936

GEORGE VI

1	11 Dec 1936-10 Dec 1937		9	11 Dec 1944-10 Dec 1945
2	11 Dec 1937-10 Dec 1938		10	11 Dec 1945-10 Dec 1946
3	11 Dec 1938-10 Dec 1939		11	11 Dec 1946-10 Dec 1947
4	11 Dec 1939-10 Dec 1940		12	11 Dec 1947-10 Dec 1948
5	11 Dec 1940-10 Dec 1941		13	11 Dec 1948-10 Dec 1949
6	11 Dec 1941-10 Dec 1942		14	11 Dec 1949-10 Dec 1950
7	11 Dec 1942-10 Dec 1943		15	11 Dec 1950-10 Dec 1951
8	11 Dec 1943-10 Dec 1944		16	11 Dec 1951- 6 Feb 1952

ELIZABETH II

1	6 Feb 1952-5 Feb 1953		24	6 Feb 1975-5 Feb 1976
2	6 Feb 1953-5 Feb 1954		25	6 Feb 1976-5 Feb 1977
3	6 Feb 1954-5 Feb 1955		26	6 Feb 1977-5 Feb 1978
4	6 Feb 1955-5 Feb 1956		27	6 Feb 1978-5 Feb 1979
5	6 Feb 1956-5 Feb 1957		28	6 Feb 1979-5 Feb 1980
6	6 Feb 1957-5 Feb 1958		29	6 Feb 1980-5 Feb 1981
7	6 Feb 1958-5 Feb 1959		30	6 Feb 1981-5 Feb 1982
8	6 Feb 1959-5 Feb 1960		31	6 Feb 1982-5 Feb 1983
9	6 Feb 1960-5 Feb 1961		32	6 Feb 1983-5 Feb 1984
10	6 Feb 1961-5 Feb 1962		33	6 Feb 1984-5 Feb 1985
11	6 Feb 1962-5 Feb 1963		34	6 Feb 1985-5 Feb 1986
12	6 Feb 1963-5 Feb 1964		35	6 Feb 1986-5 Feb 1987
13	6 Feb 1964-5 Feb 1965		36	6 Feb 1987-5 Feb 1988
14	6 Feb 1965-5 Feb 1966		37	6 Feb 1988-5 Feb 1989
15	6 Feb 1966-5 Feb 1967		38	6 Feb 1989-5 Feb 1990
16	6 Feb 1967-5 Feb 1968		39	6 Feb 1990-5 Feb 1991
17	6 Feb 1968-5 Feb 1969		40	6 Feb 1991-5 Feb 1992
18	6 Feb 1969-5 Feb 1970		41	6 Feb 1992-5 Feb 1993
19	6 Feb 1970-5 Feb 1971		42	6 Feb 1993-5 Feb 1994
20	6 Feb 1971-5 Feb 1972		43	6 Feb 1994-5 Feb 1995
21	6 Feb 1972-5 Feb 1973		44	6 Feb 1995-5 Feb 1996
22	6 Feb 1973-5 Feb 1974		45	6 Feb 1996-5 Feb 1997
23	6 Feb 1974-5 Feb 1975		46	6 Feb 1997-5 Feb 1998

> ELIZABETH II By the Grace of God of the United Kingdom of Great Britain and Northern Ireland and of Our other Realms and Territories Queen Head of the Commonwealth Defender of the Faith TO our trusty and well beloved...late Sheriff of Our County of Lancashire GREETING WHEREAS we have granted to Our trusty and well beloved...the Office of Sheriff of and within Our County of Lancashire TO HOLD AND OCCUPY the same during Our pleasure as in and by Our Letters Patent to her lately made is more fully contained WE COMMAND THAT by an Indenture between you and the said...to be duly executed you deliver to him the Rolls Writs Memoranda and all other writings to the said Office belonging in your custody WITNESS ourselves at Lancaster this 21st day of April in the forty fourth year of Our reign and in the year of our Lord one thousand nine hundred and ninety five

25. Form of words for the Writ of Assistance appointing a new sheriff for the County of Lancashire, 1995: documents such as this are among the very few which now make use of the regnal year form of dating.

POPES, BISHOPS, ABBOTS AND CHANCELLORS

The dates of popes can be found in Cheney [pp 33-39], where papal dating is explained. The *Handbook of British Chronology* lists the 'Archbishops and Bishops of England' between pages 205 and 272 with an explanatory introduction on pages 202-204 and lists of Welsh, Scottish and Irish bishops from page 273. The chancellors and keepers of the great seal are listed in the same book between pages 80 and 89. To find the names and dates of abbots is less simple. They will normally be found in whichever volume of the relevant *Victoria County History* contains the essay on 'Religious Houses', or in an authoritative work on the particular monastic house.

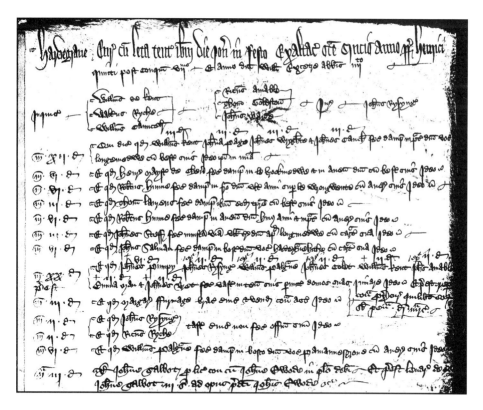

26. A court roll of the manor of Hargrave, West Suffolk (Suffolk RO E3/15.10/1.22): the heading translates as *Hargrave: Court with leet held there Thursday on the Feast of the Raising of the Holy Cross, in the 7th year of the reign of King Henry V after the Conquest, and the 4th year of Lord William of Exeter, abbot [of Bury St Edmunds]*. According to Cheney this is 14 September 1419; the *Victoria County History of Suffolk* vol.ii p.72 notes that Abbot William reigned 1415-1429.

APPENDIX 3

THE FRENCH REVOLUTIONARY CALENDAR

The revolutionary calendar was introduced in 1793 backdated to 22 Sep 1792 which became 1 Vendémiaire. The months which followed, with their first days were:

1st Vendémiaire	22 September	1 Germinal	21 March
1 Brumaire	22 October	1 Floréal	20 April
1 Frimaire	21 November	1 Prairial	20 May
1 Nivôse	21 December	1 Messidor	19 June
1 Pluviôse	20 January	1 Thermidor	19 July
1 Ventôse	19 February	1 Fructidor	18 August

Five extra days, Sanscullottides, followed in each year, with a sixth in the leap years, 1796 and 1804 *and* in 1800 which was not a leap year. So the years 1793-1805 began as follows: 1 Vendémiaire was on 22 September in 1793-5, 23 September in 1795-6, 22 September in 1796-99, 23 September in 1799-1803, 24 September in 1803-4, and 23 September in 1804-5.

The names of the months were based on the weather and the harvests in a deliberate break with Christian tradition. So Ventôse comes from *vent*, the wind, Vendémiaire from *vendage* (vintage), the grape harvest. The revolutionary calendar was abandoned by Napoleon I.

27. Destroying the traditions of the ancien regime during the early years of the French Revolution (detail of a contemporary print): all symbols of the order were the targets of attack in an attempt to obliterate most traces of the past, including coats of arms and titles (as in the picture) and the old calendar.

Appendix 4

THE CHINESE CALENDAR

The Chinese year was basically lunar, consisting of twelve months, alternately of twenty-nine and thirty days. The months are referred to by numbers and by animal names in this order: rat, ox, tiger, hare, dragon, snake, horse, sheep, monkey, fowl, dog, and pig. From ancient times the same names have been used for hours of the day and for successive years. 1996, like 1984, was the year of the Rat. The day had twelve equal periods (Shih). The first Shih beginning at midnight was called Tzu, the last ending at midnight was Hai.

The lunar calendar had 354 days; intercalary months were inserted at intervals to keep it in step with the solar year of 365 days. The Chinese solar year revolved around the equinoxes and solstices as four fixed points. The year was divided into twenty-four equal portions, Chieh. Each Chieh consisted of 15.218 days. The first Chieh in each year marked the advent of Spring. Chinese peasants regarded the Chieh as a strict timetable for farm work. The Chinese New Year begins between 21 January and 19 February in the Gregorian Calendar: in 1997, for example, on 7 February. Japan adopted the Chinese calendar in AD 604 and Korea and Vietnam also used it.

28. Festivals were central to the Chinese calendar: this detail from a hand-painted scroll depicts the Ching Ming festival at Kaifeng, capital of the Northern Sung, which celebrated the spring.

29. Two Japanese pillar clocks: the driving weight itself indicates the time as it descends slowly past a scale of hours. The Japanese did not move to the modern, or western, system of equal hours for the whole 24-hour period until 1870, but instead divided the day into six equal periods and the night into six equal periods - but day and night were not themselves the same length. The hour numerals can be adjusted to take account of this diurnal difference.

30. A Japanese striking clock: the dial rotates clockwise behind a fixed pointer and the hour marks are adjustable in a grooved ring in the dial to allow for the varying length of day and night hours over the year. Another method used in Japanese clocks to allow for variable hour length was for the clock to go at one rate during the day and another rate during the night.

THE JEWISH CALENDAR

Whitaker describes many non-Christian calendars: Hindu (p.84), Jewish (p.85), Muslim and Sikh (p.86), Coptic, Japanese and Zoroastrian (p.88). On page 9 there is a calendar with dates of the most important festivals in many religions. Only some of these non-Christian religions are likely to be of major significance to local or family historians in Britain.

The historical development of the Jewish calendar is described in Whitaker (p.85). The calendar dates events from the supposed date of the Creation which was calculated at a time 3760 years and 3 months before the beginning of the Christian era. The normal year has twelve lunar months alternatively of thirty or twenty-nine days, giving a year of 354 days. The months are Tishri (30), (C)heshvan (29), Kislev (30), Tebet (29), S(h)ebat (30), Adar (29), Nisan (30), Yiar (29), Sivan (30), Tam(m)uz (29), Ab (30), and Elul (29). This is eleven days short of the solar year, so in nineteen years the calendar would lose 209 days. To remedy this, seven times in every cycle of nineteen years an intercalary or 'embolismic' year is inserted. In Middle English 'embolism' (which means an obstruction) meant an intercalcation or insertion of a day, month or year into the calendar (e.g. 29 February in leap years). Another Adar month is put in before the normal Adar; this is Adar Rishon (first), occasionally called Ve'Adar (and Adar), to distinguish it from the normal Adar Sheni (second). Adar Rishon has 30 days, which means that in each nineteen year cycle 210 days (7 months of 30 days each) are added, almost the exactly needed correction. This happens in the 3rd, 6th, 8th, 11th, 14th, 17th and 19th years of each cycle. These years have 384 days. The requirements of the Festivals [see below] make other adjustments occasionally necessary; Cheshvan may have an extra day or Kislev lose a day. This is because the Day of Atonement is not permitted to come before or after a sabbath, for practical reasons.

The principal days in the Jewish year are:

1 & 2 Tishri	New Year/Rosh Hashana	Day of Remembrance or Judgement, because the New Year is the season of asking forgiveness for sins committed
3 Tishri	Zom (Gedaliah)	Fast of Gedaliah
10 Tishri	Yom Kippur	Fast of Atonement
15-21 Tishri	Sukkoth	Feast of Tabernacles
22 Tishri	Shemini Azereth	Feast of the 8th Day

23 Tishri	Simchath Torah	Rejoicing of the Law
25 Kislev	Hanukkah	Dedication of the Temple begins
2/3 Tebet		Dedication of the Temple ends
10 Tebet		Siege of Jerusalem. Fast
15 Shebat		New Year for Trees
13 Adar		Fast of Esther
14/15 Adar	Purim	
15-22 Nisan	Pesach	Passover
6/7 Sivan	Shabuoth	Pentecost
17 Tamuz		Taking of Jerusalem. Fast
9 Ab		Destruction of the Temple. Fast

Passover, on 15 Nisan, must not begin before the Spring equinox. The effect of the intercalation is that this never happens. In the days before the calendar was calculated, probably about 200 AD, a judgement had to be made at the previous new moon as to whether the Nissan New Moon would appear too early and, if so, the extra Adar was inserted and the real Adar postponed.

To convert Jewish dates [AM from Anno Mundi = in the year of the world's creation] into Christian years, the following formula can be used: neglect the thousands in both dating systems and add 239, from the Jewish New Year, in September/October, until 31 December, and 240 from 1 January to the Jewish New Year.

5681 AM ran from 13 September* 1920 to 2 October 1921

[681 + 239 = 920; 681 + 240 = 921]

5720 AM ran from 30 October* 1959 to 21 September 1960

[720 + 239 = 959; 720 + 240 = 960]

The Jewish year AM5757 began on 14 September 1996, the year AM5758 on 2 October 1997. Whitaker gives the dates for every Jewish month in these two years (p.85).

* Since the Jewish year changed its length, the new year began on different dates each year.

APPENDIX 6

THE MUSLIM CALENDAR

Muslims date events from the day of Mohammed's emigration from Mecca to Medina, known in Arabic as the HIJRA or HEGIRA. This was on 15 July in AD 622. The first day of the first year is 16 July AD 622 O(ld) S(tyle), 19 July N(ew) S(tyle). Muslim years are referred to in most European languages with the initials AH (After Hegira). The Muslim year has twelve lunar months, each beginning approximately with the new moon. They have, alternately, thirty and twenty-nine days, as in the Jewish calendar. The months are: Muharram (30), Safar (29), Rabi' I (30), Rabi' II (29), Jumado I (30), Jumado II (29), Rajab (30), Sha'ban (29), Ramadān (30), Shawall (Shawwāl 29), Dulkaada (Dhu'l Qa'da 30), Dulheggia (Dhu'l Hijja 29). This gives a year of 354 days, approximately 11 days less than a solar year. In every cycle of 30 years, 19 are like this, but 11 have one extra day added to the last month Dulheggia. This means that the Muslim calendar comes full cycle in relation to the solar year in about 32-5 years.

The principal days in the Muslim year are:

1 Muharram	New Year
10 Muharram	Ashura
11 Rabi' I	Birth of Mohammed
20 Jumado I	Taking of Constantinople
15 Rajab	Day of Victory
20 Rajab	Exaltation of Mohammed
15 Sha'ban	Borak's night
1, 2, 3 Shawall	Kutshuk Bairam
10 Dulheggia	Qurban

The ninth month, Ramadan, is the month of abstinence.

Currently the Muslim and Christian calendars relate as follows:

1 Muharram 1416 = Wednesday 3 May 1995

1 Muharram 1417 = Sunday 19 May 1996

1 Muharram 1418 = Friday 9 May 1997

1 Muharram 1419 = Tuesday 28 April 1998

1 Muharram 1420 = Saturday 17 April 1999

1 Muharram 1421 = Thursday 6 April 2000

The Muslim year 1416 is in the forty-eighth cycle of thirty years. Whitaker gives the dates of every month for the years AH 1417 and AH 1418 (p.86).

THE CHRISTIAN FEASTS IN RELATION TO THE DATE OF EASTER SUNDAY

The majority of Christian feasts bear the same relationship to the date of Easter in every year. They change with the changes in the date of Easter. Since this could move between March 22 and April 25 there were changes in the numbers of Christian feasts at the beginning and end of the year. At the beginning of the year there could be between one and six Epiphany Sundays. Towards the end of the year there could be between twenty-seven and twenty-two Trinity Sundays. The other feasts were standard. To calculate the date in a particular year on which any feast fell, find the date of Easter from Cheney's tables [pp 156-161] and count the days backwards and forwards from Easter Sunday, in accordance with this Table.

31. Palm Sunday celebrations: in many places Palm Sunday processions were held, to symbolise Christ's entry into Jerusalem when his path was strewn with palm branches.

Days before Easter		Days after Easter	
64	Septuagesima	1	EASTER SUNDAY
57	Sexagesima	8	Quasimodo
50	Quinquagesima	15	Easter 2
48	Shrove Tuesday	22	Easter 3
47	Ash Wednesday	29	Easter 4
43	Quadregesima	36	Rogation
40	Ember	40	Ascension
38	Ember	43	Ascension 1
37	Ember	50	Whit Sunday
36	Lent 2	53	Ember
29	Lent 3	55	Ember
22	Lent 4	56	Ember
15	Passion	57	Trinity
8	Palm Sunday	61	Corpus Christi
3	Good Friday	64	Trinity 1
1	EASTER SUNDAY		Trinity 2-22 the following Sundays, at 7 day intervals

Ash Wednesday is the first day of Lent, and the five Sundays of Lent follow: Quadragesima is the first, and Passion Sunday is the fifth Sunday of Lent.

253	Advent 1
260	Advent 2
267	Advent 3
270	Ember
272	Ember
273	Ember
274	Advent 4

Ember Days were originally additional fast days. The name is derived from the Old English *ymbryne*, a circuit, because of their place in the annual cycle of church feasts. There are three further Ember days on the Wednesday, Friday and Saturday in the third week of September. The additional Epiphany and Trinity Sundays occur when Easter Sunday falls as follows:

22-24 March	:	1	Epiphany Sunday			
22-26 March	:	27	Trinity Sundays			
25-31 March	:	2	Epiphanies	27 March - 2 April	:	26 Trinitys
1-7 April	:	3	Epiphanies	3-9 April	:	25 Trinitys
8-14 April	:	4	Epiphanies	10-16 April	:	24 Trinitys
15-21 April	:	5	Epiphanies	17-23 April	:	23 Trinitys
22-25 April	:	6	Epiphanies	24-25 April	:	22 Trinitys

In Whitaker (p.83) there is a table of 'Movable Feasts' covering the years 1997-2029 which gives the changing dates of Ash Wednesday, Easter, Ascension, Pentecost (Whit Sunday) and Advent Sunday.

APPENDIX 8

THE ORTHODOX YEAR

Since AD 312, when the Roman emperor Constantine introduced indictions of fifteen years, which began on 1 September, for tax purposes, the Orthodox Church has begun its years on that day. The Orthodox Church has an ecclesiastical year which differs from the Roman year, but like the Roman year it is focused around the date of Easter. It has accepted the Gregorian calendar for fixed feasts, but uses the Julian calendar for movable feasts. This is why the date of Easter differs in the two churches. There are four periods of fast and twelve great feasts as well as Easter. Many of the same saints' days are celebrated in the two churches but the Orthodox Church has many more.[42]

MEDIEVAL HOLY DAYS

In 1362 Archbishop Simon Islip named the following days and feasts as holy days, on which no work should be done.

25 December	Christmas
26 December	St Stephen
27 December	St John the Evangelist
28 December	Holy Innocents
29 December	St Thomas the Martyr
1 January	Circumcision
6 January	Epiphany
2 February	Purification of the Blessed Virgin Mary
24/25 February	St Matthias
25 March	Annunciation of the Blessed Virgin Mary
	Easter and the three following days
25 April	St Mark
1 May	SS Philip and James
3 May	Discovery of the Holy Cross
	Ascension [see Appendix 7]
	Whit Sunday and the three following days [see Appendix 7]
	Corpus Christi [see Appendix 7]
24 June	Nativity of St John the Baptist
29 June	SS Peter and Paul
7 July	Translation of St Thomas the Martyr
22 July	St Mary Magdalene
25 July	St James
10 August	St Lawrence
15 August	Assumption of the Blessed Virgin Mary
24 August	St Bartholomew
8 September	Nativity of the Blessed Virgin Mary
14 September	Exaltation of the cross
21 September	St Matthew
29 September	St Michael
18 October	St Luke
28 October	SS Simon and Jude
1 November	All Saints

30 November	St Andrew
6 December	St Nicholas
8 December	Conception of the Blessed Virgin Mary
21 December	St Thomas the Apostle
All Sundays	

St George [23 April] was added to the list in the fifteenth century.[43]

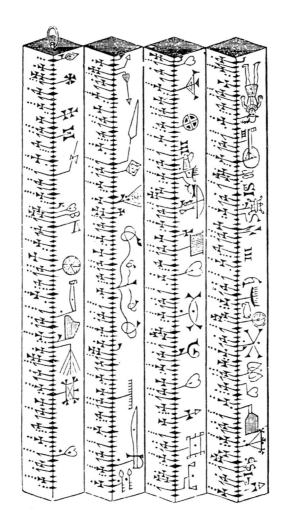

32. A 'clog almanac': this is a square hardwood stick (all four faces being shown in this drawing) with days marked by notches at the corners. Sundays are distinguished by broader cuts. The feasts were denoted by appropriate symbols, such as a harp for St David's Day on 1 March. It was about eight inches long and could either be hung up in the parlour for reference or carried as part of a walking cane.

Appendix 10

THE ROMAN MONTHS

The Roman months, and the origins of the names, were as follows:

January	Janus, god of openings
February	Februa, the feast of expiation
March	Mars, the god of war
April	either the verb *aperire*, to open, because it is when trees and flowers open, or from Aphrile, or Aphrodite
May	the goddess, Maia
June	the goddess, Juno
Quintilis	Quintus, 5th (when the year began in March)
Sextilus	Sextus, 6th
September	Septem = 7
October	Octo = 8
November	Novem = 9
December	Decem = 10

The months Quintilis and Sextilus were renamed July and August in honour of Julius Caesar and Augustus Caesar. Common abbreviations for the last four months in English documents before the 18th century were: 7^{ber} = September; 8^{ber} = October; 9^{ber} = November, and 10^{ber} = December; these can mislead the unwary student.

Roman months were divided into three periods by Calends, Nones and Ides. The Calends was the first day of the month. The Ides were eight days earlier and the Nones either four or six days later. The days between these three were counted as follows: between the Calends and Nones the days were numbered downwards to Nones. So 1 January = Calends; 2 January = 4 Nones; 3 January = 3 Nones; 4 January = 2 Nones; and 5 January = Nones. Then came days counted downwards to the Ides. So 6 January = 8 Ides and 13 January = Ides. The Calends then began with the odd result, for us today, that what we call 14 January was in the calendar 19 Calends of February! The Nones in March, May, July and October were on the 7th of the month. The number of Calends' days varied.

January 19	April 18	July 17	October 17
February* 16	May 17	August 19	November 18
March 17	June 18	September 18	December 19

* in leap years there were two 6 Calends on 24th and 25th

Whitaker (p.89) prints in parallel calendars of the 'Present days of the month' and of the equivalent Kalends, Nones and Ides for two groups of 31 days months, for the 30 days months, and for February.

33. Julius Caesar: the system of measuring time which was created by the reform of the Roman calendar under Julius Caesar survived in southern Europe until further reforms in the 16th century, and in northern Europe until the mid-18th century.

QUAKER DATING

Valerie Norrington has explained, in a most useful article [see Bibliography], the complexities of Quaker dating. Quakers would not use the pagan names either of days of the month or of months. They used numbers. Sunday was the first day, 1st day, or 1d, or 1. An Aldeburgh (Suffolk) meeting was minuted: 'Our next Monethly Meeting to bee at Hannah Peirsons the 2d 2d Day of next Moneth'. It was held 'on the second second day, or second Monday, of April'. In Quaker registers 'the year is given first, followed by the month and then the day. Beware not to confuse 1699.5.12 for the 5th of the 12th month, because it is the 12th of the 5th month'.

There is a special problem in making sure that the student interprets accurately Quaker dates from before 1752. While Old Style dating [see pp 25-26] was in operation in England the Quakers numbered the months from March, which was 'first month'. This, incidentally, had the effect that their numbers were the same as the Roman names, ie December was 10th month to the Quakers [see p 78] January and February became the 11th and 12th months of the year. However, just to make life difficult the Quakers chose to begin the new year on 1 March. Valerie Norrington quotes a Sussex register: 'by the account in this Booke the year is to Begin the First day of the First Month comonly called March. Whereas in the worlds [ie non-Quakers] Account it begins not untill the 25th day of the said month'. 'By adding two to the number of the month given in a Quaker Register, prior to January 1752, it is possible to arrive at the actual month'.[44] From 1 January 1752, January became the first month and December the twelfth.

APPENDIX 12

A CALENDAR OF INSTITUTIONAL DATES

What follows are the modern dates of the beginning and end of the Law and Oxbridge terms. Full terms in the two universities are only of eight weeks' duration. In 1996 for example the Cambridge Full Term began on 16 January and ended on 15 March, while Lent Term ended on 24 March. The Oxford Full Term began on 14 January and ended on 9 March, while Hilary Term only ended on 25 March.

5 January	Cambridge Lent Term begins
7 January	Oxford Hilary Term begins
Between 15 & 21 Jan	Hilary Law Term begins
2 February	SCOTTISH QUARTER DAY, Candlemas
Between 6 & 13 Feb	Hilary Law Term ends
Between 18 & 25 Mar	Oxford Hilary Term ends
Between 24 & 25 Mar	Cambridge Lent term ends
25 March	ENGLISH QUARTER DAY. Lady Day
Between 5 Apr & 2 May	Easter Law Term begins
Between 10 & 17 Apr	Cambridge Easter Term begins
Between 20 & 25 Apr	Oxford Trinity Term begins
Between 27 Apr & 24 May	Easter Law Term ends
15 May	SCOTTISH QUARTER DAY. Whitsun
Between 18 & 25 Jun	Cambridge Easter Term ends
24 Jun	ENGLISH QUARTER DAY. Midsummer Day. Nativity of St John Baptist
Between 1 & 7 Jul	Trinity Law Term begins
6 July	Oxford Trinity Term ends
Between 23 & 29 Jul	Trinity Law Term ends
1 August	SCOTTISH QUARTER DAY. Lammas
29 September	ENGLISH QUARTER DAY. Michaelmas
1 October	Cambridge and Oxford Michaelmas Terms begin
Between 1 & 2 Nov	Michaelmas Law Term begins
11 November	SCOTTISH QUARTER DAY. Martinmas

Between 23 & 29 Nov	Michaelmas Law Term ends
Between 17 & 19 Dec	Oxford Michaelmas Term ends
19 December	Cambridge Michaelmas Term ends
25 December	ENGLISH QUARTER DAY. Christmas Day

There is supplementary information in Whitaker (p.87), and in its 'Astronomy' section Whitaker has a 'calendar for each month [which] shows dates of religious, civil and legal significance'. These have invaluable historical information, particularly of the dates of birth and death of well-known people.

NOTES AND REFERENCES

1 E. P. Thompson, 'Time, Work-Discipline, and Industrial Capitalism', in *Past and Present*, no. 38 (Dec 1967), p. 67

2 D. Landes, *Revolution in Time: Clocks and the Making of the Modern World* (Harvard U.P., 1938), p. 1

3 D. Whitelock (ed.), *The Anglo-Saxon Chronicle, a revised translation* (Eyre & Spottiswood, 1961-5), p. xxiv

4 Steinberg, pp. 115 and 116; Elton, pp. 111-112 and 292; Scarisbrick, pp. 309, 483 and 555

5 G. D. H. Cole, *A short history of the British working-class movement 1789-1940* (p. 240), and *The Common People* (pp. 422 and 712)

6 See Whitaker, p. 96

7 C. Tickell, 'Climate and History', in *Oxford Today*, vol. 8, no. 2 (Hilary 1996), pp. 27-30; for further information see the *Cambridge Encyclopaedia of Archaeology*

8 C. A. Hewett, *The development of carpentry: an Essex study* (David and Charles, 1969), p. 21

9 E. H. Blakeney (ed.), *A smaller Classical dictionary* (Dent, 1910, 1928 edition), pp. 589-590

10 Whitby is the accepted location of Streoneshalh, the placename used by Bede. The date of the Synod of Whitby is an example of the confusion in historical records, which I have discussed on pp. 00. Bede described the year as 664. In his *Anglo-Saxon England* (Oxford U.P., 1943, p. 129) F. M. Stenton has explained why the date, in modern chronology, should be 663.

11 Whitaker has two tables which give the same information in different ways. 'Easter Days and Dominical Letters 1500-2033' is on p. 84, and a 'Calendar for 1780-2033' on pp. 90-93. The latter contains the fourteen possible different calendars - seven of which are for leap years - with the relevant dates of Easter to which they apply, but without the church festivals which Cheney's calendars contain.

12 Whitaker (p. 83) has a list of the dates of movable feasts from 1997 to 2029

13 Whitaker has a useful simple definition on p. 81: 'Measurements of time are based on the time taken by the earth to rotate on its axis (day); by the moon to revolve round the earth (month); and by the earth to revolve round the sun (year). From these, which are not commensurable, certain average of mean intervals have been adopted for ordinary use'. The day, the month and the year are described in what follows.

14 See Whitaker, p. 88

15 Whitelock, *op. cit.*, p. xxiv

16 See Whitaker, p. 86

17 R. Poole, '"Give us our eleven days": calendar reform in eighteenth century England', in *Past and Present*, no. 149 (Nov 1995), p. 110

18 Poole, *op. cit.*, pp. 98, 105, 127, 138 and 139

19 G. J. Whitrow, *Time in History* (Oxford U.P., 1988), p. 15

20 See Whitaker, p. 75

21 Poole, *op. cit.*, p. 96

22 J. M. Synge, *Plays, Poems and Prose* (Everyman, 1941), p. 257

23 Landes, *op. cit.*, pp. 63 and 77-8

24 Thompson, *op. cit.*, p. 63

25 Landes, *op. cit.*, p. 83

26 F. Steer, *Farm and cottage inventories of mid-Essex 1635-1749* (Essex County Council, 1950), p. 20

27 A. Milward and S. B. Saul, *The economic development of Continental Europe 1780-1870* (Allen & Unwin, 1973), pp. 459-60

28 Lancashire Record Office, DDHK (uncatalogued)

29 see Whitaker, p. 87

30 M. Powicke and E. B. Fryde, *Handbook of British Chronology* (Royal Historical Society, 1961), pp. 492-497, 526-534, and 535-544

31 D. and G. Butler, *British political facts 1900-1985* (Macmillan, 1986), pp. 192 and 176

32 Poole, *op. cit.*, p. 139

33 C. Phythian Adams, *Local history and folklore* (Standing Conference for Local History, 1975), p. 21

34 M. Baker, *Folklore and customs of rural England* (David and Charles, 1974), p. 89

35 R. Hutton, *The Stations of the Sun: a history of the ritual year in Britain* (Oxford U.P., 1996), p. 135

36 A. R. Wright (ed. By T. E. Lones), *British Calendar Customs, England: vol 3, Fixed Festivals, June to December* (Folklore Society, 1940), p. 150

37 Wright, *op. cit.*, p. 181

38 Phythian Adams, *op. cit.*, pp. 21 and 24

39 D. Wilkins, *Concilia*, vol. 3 (1737), p. 823

40 Whitrow, *op. cit.*, p. 167

41 L. Munby (ed.), *Life and death in Kings Langley: wills and inventories 1498-1659* (Kings Langley Local History & Museum Society, 1981), p. 34

42 C. Arnold Baker and A. Dent, *Everyman's Dictionary of Dates* (1954) pp. xxi-xxiv

43 W. Lyndwood, *Provinciale* (Oxford, 1969), pp. 101-2 and 103

44 V. Norrington, 'The first month called March: the dating of Quaker documents', in *Suffolk Review*, new series no. 27 (1996), pp. 15, 17 and 14

BIBLIOGRAPHY

The editions listed are those which I have consulted, not necessarily either the first or the latest.

C. Arnold-Baker & A. Dent, *Everyman's Dictionary of Dates*. Dent. 1954

D. Attwater, *Penguin Dictionary of Saints*. 2nd ed., updated by C. R. John. Penguin. 1983

M. Baker, *Folklore & Customs of Rural England*. David and Charles. 1974

E.H. Blakeney (ed.), *A Smaller Classical Dictionary*. Dent. 1910. 1928 ed.

J. Brand, *Popular Antiquities*. 3 vols. Charles Knight. 1841-2

D. and G. Butler, *British Political Facts 1900-1985*. Macmillan. 1986

C.R. Cheney, *Handbook of Dates for Students of English History*. Royal Historical Society, 1945. 1970 with corrections

G. D.H. Cole & R. Postgate, *The Common People 1746-1946*. Methuen 1964

G.D.H. Cole, *Short History of the British Working-Class Movement 1789-1947*. Allen & Unwin. 1948

G.R. Elton, *Reform and Reformation: England 1509-1558*. Arnold. 1977

C.A. Hewett, *The Development of Carpentry 1200-1700: an Essex Study*. David and Charles. 1969

C.A. Hewett, *Church Carpentry: a study based on Essex Examples*. Phillimore. 1974

D. Howse, *Greenwich Time*. OUP. 1980

R. Hutton, *The Rise and Fall of Merry England: the ritual year 1400-1700*. OUP. 1994

R. Hutton, *The Stations of the Sun: a history of the ritual year in Britain*. OUP. 1996

W. Hone, *Every Day Book*

    Vol 1. Hunt & Clarke 1826, reprint Ward, Lock 1888

    Vol 2. Hunt & Clarke 1827, reprint Ward, Lock 1889

W. Hone, *Table Book*. Hunt & Clarke 1827, reprint William Tegg 1878

W. Hone, *Year Book*. Thomas Tegg 1832, reprint Ward, Lock 1892

D.S. Landes, *Revolution in Time: Clocks and the Making of the Modern World*. Harvard UP. 1983

H. Marsden (ed.), *Whitaker's Almanack 1997* (J. Whitaker & Sons, 1996)

A. Milward & S. B. Saul, *The Economic Development of Continental Europe 1780-1870*. Allen & Unwin. 1973

L.M. Munby (ed.), *Life and Death in Kings Langley: wills and inventories 1498-1659*. Kings Langley Local History and Museum Society. 1981

V. Norrington, 'The First Month called March: the dating of Quaker Documents' in *Suffolk Review*. New Series 27. 1996

C. Phythian Adams, *Local History and Folklore*. Standing Conference for Local History. 1975

R. Poole, '"Give us our eleven days": Calendar Reform in eighteenth century England' in *Past and Present* No 149, Nov 1995

E. Porter, *Cambridgeshire Customs and Folklore*. Routledge. 1969

F.M. Powicke & E. B. Fryde (eds.), *Handbook of British Chronology*. Royal Historical Society. 1961

J. Scarisbrick, *Henry VIII*. Penguin. 1971

Francis Steer, *Farm and Cottage Inventories of Mid-Essex 1635–1749*. Essex County Council. 1950

S.H. Steinberg, *Historical Tables 58 BC – AD 1965*. Macmillan. 8th ed. 1966

F.M. Stenton, *Anglo-Saxon England*. OUP. 1943

J. Strutt, *Sports and Pastimes of the People of England* (1801). William Tegg. 1850

J.M. Synge, *Plays, Poems, and Prose*. Everyman. 1941

T.F. Thiselton-Dyer, *British Popular Customs*. Bell. 1876

E.P. Thompson, 'Time, Work-Discipline, and Industrial Capitalism' in *Past and Present* No 38, Dec 1967

C. Tickell, 'Climate and History' in *Oxford Today* Vol 8, No 2. Hilary issue 1996. pp 27-30

D. Whitelock (ed.), *The Anglo-Saxon Chronicle, a revised translation*. Eyre & Spottiswoode. 1961-1965

G.J. Whitrow, *Time in History*. OUP. 1988

D. Wilkins, *Concilia* Vol 3. 1737

A.R. Wright, T. E. Lones (ed.), *British Calendar Customs, England*.

   Vol 1: *Movable Festivals*. Folklore Society. 1936

   Vol 2: *Fixed Festivals, January-May*. Folklore Society. 1938

   Vol 3: *Fixed Festivals, June-December*. Folklore Society. 1940